The Far East Comes Near

Home is on the river (Saigon).
Photo by Le Van Khoa.

The Far East Comes Near

Autobiographical Accounts of

Southeast Asian Students

in America

Edited by

Lucy Nguyen-Hong-Nhiem and

Joel Martin Halpern

The University of Massachusetts Press

Amherst

Printed in the United States of America
LC 88–32687
ISBN 0–87023–671–7 (cloth); 672–5 (pbk.)
Designed by Barbara Werden
Set in Linotron Plantin at Keystone Typesetting
Printed by Thomson-Shore and bound by John Dekker & Sons

Library of Congress Cataloging-in-Publication Data
The Far East comes near: autobiographical accounts of Southeast Asian students in America/edited by Lucy Nguyen-Hong-Nhiem and Joel Martin Halpern.
p. cm.
ISBN 0–87023–671–7—ISBN 0–87023–672–5 (pbk.)
1. Indochinese—Education (Higher)—United States. 2. Indochinese—United States—Biography. 3. Refugees—Indochina. 4. Refugees—United States. I. Nguyen, Lucy Hong Nhiem, 1939– . II. Halpern, Joel Martin.
LC2633.6.F37 1989
378′.1982—dc19 88–32687
CIP

British Library Cataloguing in Publication data are available.

Contents

Student Essays from Vietnam*

*The essays have been arranged within an implicit chronological framework. Thus those that focus on life in the home countries come first and are followed by those that deal with the manner of escape and, finally, the experiences in America.

Student Essays from Cambodia

Student Essays from Laos

List of Illustrations

Acknowledgments

We would like to thank the Bilingual Collegiate Program of the University of Massachusetts at Amherst for providing funds to type the manuscript and especially Nguyen Quoc Tuan for untiringly doing the tedious computer entry. Julie Rapoport prepared the initial draft of Notes on the Authors and as an academic adviser worked with the students in preparing their English-language essays. Kathleen Mullins was very helpful with the preliminary editing of these essays. Barbara Kerewsky-Halpern provided many valuable editorial suggestions at various stages in the development of the manuscript. Above all we are indebted to our students for sharing their life experiences as they were learning about Southeast Asian cultures in an academic context and for educating us about ways of survival in adapting to diversity.

LUCY NGUYEN-HONG-NHIEM
JOEL MARTIN HALPERN

Foreword

FROM the 1800s to the present, the peoples of Asia have immigrated to the United States for many of the same reasons as other immigrant groups: to escape poverty or political oppression and to find better economic opportunities and freedom of expression.

Since the 1965 immigration law did away with exclusionary quotas, the number of Americans of Asian extraction has quintupled to more than five million, or about 2 percent of the population. The first immigrants after 1965 were mostly middle-class professionals from Hong Kong, Taiwan, South Korea, India, and the Philippines. In 1975, at the end of the Vietnam War, 130,000 refugees, mostly from the educated middle class, began arriving. Three years later, a second group of 650,000 Indochinese, mostly from rural areas and refugee camps, followed.* And the numbers are still growing. By the year 2000, there will be another doubling of the Asian-American population, to ten million or more.

Yet the enormity of these statistics and the generalization of the label "Asian American" mask the diversity of the individuals who swell these numbers. Religious as well as economic backgrounds differ. Some are Buddhist, others Confucian or Catholic. Some, like Lam Phu, were fortunate to come with their entire family intact; others, like Ta Minh Tri, arrive alone without the emotional support of kin.

*David Brand, "The New Whiz Kids," *Time*, August 31, 1987, p. 42.

Listen to the voices of these new Americans. Their stories are chilling, poignant but full of hope. Vietnamese, Laotian, or Cambodian, they share many of the same ancient Asian values: discipline, reverence of family, and a deep respect for education. These values seem peculiarly compatible with the Protestant work ethic.

Like their predecessors, these latest Southeast Asian immigrants feel an enormous pressure to excel, which is coupled with an equally strong desire to prove themselves in their newly adopted country. Many will be more than equal to the task, but for every Westinghouse Science scholar and valedictorian, there is a young person of average or below average ability. Each deserves to be nurtured. Each has a unique contribution to make. Each must make his or her own way.

We have an obligation to our new American brothers and sisters, as Ervin Staub suggests, to reach out to them, to extend our acceptance and hospitality. While affirming our common humanity, we should appreciate their cultural differences. Rather than rush to assimilate them, let us learn from them as we share our own best selves.

DEIRDRE LING

The Far East Comes Near

JOEL MARTIN HALPERN

Introduction

THIS book contains autobiographical essays by students originally from Vietnam, Cambodia, and Laos, all of whom arrived in this country as refugees between 1975 and 1982. The essays were written in conjunction with a Southeast Asian cultures course at the University of Massachusetts taught jointly by Lucy Nguyen-Hong-Nhiem and me since 1984. The student contributors are among the approximately one million Southeast Asians who have come from Indochina to the United States since 1975.

American history is replete with traumatic migrations. We began with optimistic Pilgrims and Quakers seeking freedom of conscience, as well as with Africans in bondage. In the nineteenth century there were starving Irish and, later, oppressed southern and eastern Europeans seeking hope and economic survival. A later wave of Armenians fleeing the Turkish-imposed genocide during World War I sought America as a place of refuge, as did the Jewish survivors of the World War II Holocaust.

But never, until 1975 with the collapse of the Indochina governments, did Asians arrive in America in massive numbers, their migration the result of an imperial war in which America entered with limited aims and was defeated.* The earlier migrations of Chinese,

*According to the Office of Refugee Resettlement, as of 1988 the number of Southeast Asian immigrants in the United States was 856,500. Overall there are 1,523,900 known to be living abroad, of whom 114,400 are in Canada, 113,200 in Australia, and 103,000 in France. The exodus to the West is continuing; thus in March 1988, 5,908 Indochinese left Southeast Asia, of which number 3,899 came to the United States.

Japanese, and Pilipinos took place over a much longer period. The Indochinese reaching the United States since 1975 are part of a large-scale migration of many non-European and Asian peoples. The largest numbers seeking sanctuary have been those fleeing their homelands in this hemisphere, many of them refugees from revolutions and military and civilian violence—Cubans, Salvadorans, Guatemalans, Haitians, Chileans, and Nicaraguans—but the list also includes Lebanese, Iranians, and others escaping the violence in the Middle East, and smaller numbers of such groups as Afghans, Ethiopians, and Somalians fleeing conflicts in their native lands.

The recent Indochinese refugees join fellow Asians who have come for mixed economic and political reasons—Pilipinos, Taiwanese, Koreans, Indians, and Sri Lankans. According to some census projections, by the year 2000 no group, including those specifically of west European origin, the original immigrant groups, will be a clear majority of the U.S. population. The Indochinese immigrants of the late 1970s and the 1980s are thus entering an America very different from that of earlier generations of Asian immigrants. If compared to Hispanics, Asians are a numerically small group in the United States, but they are nonetheless a prominent part of the American ethnic mosaic. The America of the 1930s and 1940s with its Oriental exclusion acts, legal restrictions on intermarriage, ghettoization in Chinatowns, and, perhaps most significantly, the internment of Japanese Americans during World War II is now receding from memory. The change is exemplified by the fact that bilingual education and official multilingualism have already become significant political issues in some states. This changing sociocultural environment is reflected in some of the student essays in this book.

One should be aware of the important cultural distinctions among the Indochinese immigrants. These differences have affected reasons for migration and the nature of adaptation to American society. The term "Indochinese," referring to a portion of the inhabitants of mainland Southeast Asia, is used here as shorthand. It is in some ways equivalent to the term "Balkan" used to identify the peoples of southeast Europe. Like the Greeks, Albanians, and South Slavs who each have distinct linguistic, cultural, and historical traditions and an accompanying history of conflict, the Vietnamese, Cambodian, and Lao peoples each have separate histories, which include recurrent struggles. In addition, both the Balkan peoples and the Indochinese have endured ex-

High school girls (Hué, Perfume River).
Photo by Le Van Khoa.

tended periods of colonialism. In the case of the Indochinese, the very term is linked to the history of the French colonial presence which developed in the middle of the nineteenth century and lasted nearly a hundred years. "Indochina" was a French colonial creation. It never existed as a political entity before or after independence. The term is used here in a geographic sense, but it also represents an area with a shared history amidst cultural diversity.

While all the peoples of Indochina were strongly affected by events in China, Vietnamese culture has been most profoundly shaped by them. This influence is particularly evident in the Confucian heritage in Vietnamese familial and political structures but can also be seen in their art, language, and literature.

On the other hand, Cambodia and Laos in their political and religious structures have been most clearly influenced by contacts with India. The very name Indochina, of course, implies this mix of cultural influences. But while Cambodia and Laos do share a common religious, artistic, and sociopolitical heritage, their histories and ethnic structuring are distinct. Khmer and Lao are mutually unintelligible; Laos is mountainous and lacks the flat plains of Cambodia whose productive irrigated rice agriculture made possible the growth of a massive medieval state symbolized by the remains of Angkor, which even today continue to be the preeminent national symbol.

In both Vietnam and Cambodia, tribal groups constitute a small minority of the total population. In Laos, however, tribal peoples of the uplands have historically been about half the total population. Finally, the cultural and linguistic ties of the Lao are with the Thai. The Mekong River border divides a single people. Their separation is a result of a border established by the expansion of French colonial power in the nineteenth century which created a Lao political entity, but the Lao of Laos and the ethnic Lao of northern and northeast Thailand continue to share a common cultural tradition.

Religion is also significant. Buddhism, which entered Indochina overseas from India, exists in all three countries. Although Buddhist practice in present-day Vietnam is linked to that of China, the important initial contacts came from India.* Vietnam is a country of many faiths, which distinguishes it from the other countries, where

*Keith Weller Taylor, *The Birth of Vietnam* (Berkeley: University of California Press, 1983), 80–84.

Buddhism is the dominant religion. Perhaps the most lasting, if limited, impact of French colonial influence was the work of the Catholic missionaries in Vietnam, for some 10 percent of Vietnamese remain Catholic today. Many from Vietnam who have come to the United States have become part of the American Catholic community, in some cases with their own priests and parishes.

The recent emigrants from Southeast Asia have encountered an America that has changed from its earlier religious narrowness. This transformation is an aspect of the transcultural process implied in the concept of the far world coming near. Let me give a personal example.

As an employee of the American Aid Program, I was stationed from 1956 to 1958 in Luang Prabang, the then-royal capital in northern Laos. During that time I had the unique opportunity of observing life there and in the peaceful countryside, where it was possible to travel without hindrance. I grew accustomed to the ever-present sight of Buddhist stupas (conical religious structures which contain Buddhist images) forming the skyline. I also heard daily the sounds of temple drums signaling the morning parade through the town of saffron-robed monks with their bowls, accepting the offerings of rice from the women townsfolk who enhanced their religious stature by their donations. Now, every morning when I drive to work in Amherst I can see from the top of my hill the massive stupa of a Buddhist temple compound recently erected on a rise in the neighboring town of Leverett.

This stupa is part of a religious complex that includes residences for monks and nuns and buildings for meditation. It was erected by Japanese Buddhist monks and a group of American supporters. The resident monks and nuns (including some Americans) do not go with their empty rice bowls to the small Leverett village center or to larger Amherst, but at the time of religious holidays such as the Buddhist New Year, the Leverett setting is a gathering place for Buddhists from New England and New York. Especially prominent are those who have recently come from south and Southeast Asia. At these times one can find food prepared by the local Cambodian community or Sri Lankan delicacies made by visitors from New York's Staten Island. How appropriate to come to this historic closure in New England, for it is from this part of America, as early as the 1820s, that the first missionaries were sent to Burma, well before Manifest Destiny closed in on the Indians of the American West.

Similar processes of change have also affected Saint Brigid's Catholic Church in the center of Amherst. Here the Vietnamese mid-autumn festival dragon is not a stranger. A parade staged on Pleasant Street, Amherst's main thoroughfare, by the Vietnamese Students' Association of the University of Massachusetts ends in the church's social hall to celebrate a meeting of the Vietnamese Cultural Asssociation. This church has also been host to wedding ceremonies conducted in Vietnamese by Vietnamese priests. At the same time, in Lowell, Massachusetts, young Cambodian men are ordained as monks during the period of their summer vacation and older women choose to become nuns, for a period, at the community's local Buddhist temple. Others make traditional kites to fly at the time of the Buddhist New Year.

There are clear similarities between the experiences of the Indochinese and earlier generations of immigrants. For some, the process of assimilation has been mixed with violence and grief; others experience personal successes. Some become lost in the new environment and others are able to participate in communities that preserve cultural heritages. The violence of nativist bigotry has never been absent from the American scene, although it has been usually a minor theme. It becomes acute when there is competition for jobs and housing or when favoritism is perceived in connection with government-sponsored resettlement programs. Indochinese in Massachusetts have been the victims of harassment, house burnings, and even murder. Ethnic conflicts in the Boston area recall the earlier treatment of Irish immigrants in the nineteenth and early twentieth centuries and attitudes toward those who came from southern and eastern Europe during the last hundred years.

Part of the somber aspect of the Indochinese refugee experience in America is the psychic toll exacted. The traumas of the war, flight, and the immigrant experience in America become manifest in mental disturbances, which have sometimes led to suicide or even murder of close kin. These situations occur when contradictions in values become insupportable or as a result of the constant conflicts in the struggle for achievement in the new land. The successful are able to fulfill the stereotype of Asian exceptionalism now given wide publicity, but those who fail are also becoming more apparent. As Deirdre Ling notes, we must concern ourselves with those who experience difficulty at the same time that we commend the achievers.

The essays reflect the students' mixed situation, but for the most part they do not focus on current problems. The students show a built-in sense of caution. Their memories of personal disasters in their homelands are still fresh, and although they exhibit an obvious concern with their present situation, it is the horrors of war and the pain of uprooting that they first must confront. Leaving one's homeland and native culture with the irreversible severing of ties with family, kin, and friends is an unforgettable step. It may be possible that some will be able to return for a visit but this is never certain and cannot be considered at the time of departure. (This sense of finality is in contrast to the situation of economic migrants such as those from Mexico where a type of commuting situation may exist or a permanent return home may be assumed, even if it never comes about.) For many if not most Indochinese, the experience is closest to that of the Jews who fled persecution in Europe or to that of the Armenians who escaped from Turkey. Arrival in America meant survival in the most elemental sense. The ritual of transition symbolized by the epic journey of escape takes on great importance. The film *The Killing Fields* portrays the experience of Dith Pran. It presents aspects of the Cambodian experience that were shared by many—a journey from the charnel house of death that the regime of Pol Pot created after coming to power in 1975.

At the other extreme from the Khmer situation was the experience of many Lao. While they knew the trauma of leaving their home, they had only the Mekong to cross, although this crossing could be risky and was sometimes accompanied by a hail of bullets. A little more than a decade after flight, one of the Lao students whose essay appears in this volume journeyed to northeast Thailand with her mother. She did not cross over into Laos but her relatives came to Thailand for an elaborate Buddhist celebration. It appears that such return visits will be increasing.

The policies of the Vietnamese Communist government were not as destructive as those of the Pol Pot regime. They could, however, be draconian for the families of those who had been associated with the South Vietnamese government—former officials or army officers or employees of the Americans. Loss of property and position was to be expected but harder to bear was the imprisonment of family heads in reeducation camps from which release was not certain. For some, more severe events had occurred earlier when family members, usually fathers and brothers, were killed in the war. Violent death of loved ones is a common experience cited in these essays.

Among the Vietnamese student essays, the experiences of

the "boat people" are most commonly portrayed. Unlike the Khmer who were fleeing a society in disintegration, where to remain often meant to die, the Vietnamese were escaping a country that had stabilized, albeit with a strongly perceived level of oppression.

The escape of the Vietnamese boat people was complicated and involved many people. A relatively large boat was necessary, although these ships were frequently in poor shape for a long sea voyage. Obtaining a boat meant money and organization and the stockpiling of fuel and supplies. Funds were often paid, in advance, from the United States to organizers in Vietnam. A crew was also required, even if the members lacked extensive seafaring skills. Precise planning, secrecy, and concealment were necessary. All these factors provided elements of drama, as did the final consultations with family members. Some of the essays describe the selections that were made of who should go and who should stay.

During the voyage, death by drowning and through violence at the hands of Thai pirates were real possibilities. We obviously don't have the accounts of those who were lost at sea nor do we know with accuracy the odds for survival, but both the sense of hope and the fears of death are emphasized in these student accounts, and there is one describing how a young woman was victimized.

For the lucky ones, safe landing and subsequent arrival at a refugee camp ended the boat trip which was the second phase of the personal epic that began with the initial uprooting. Then followed the next stage, the long struggle for a return to "normalcy," with migration to a permanent home: a new norm, a new status, one that can never be equivalent to the old one, but one that does represent the reestablishment and renewal of self in a new sociocultural framework. Involved is a process of planning and building, the inverse of the beginning of the epic that chronicles the debasement and progressive destruction of a way of life. For many of the students this earlier experience involved the shattering of a childhood never fully realized. This process is particularly poignant in those Cambodian essays that describe life in labor camps for very young children of five or six. The death rates were obviously enormous and the efficacy of these infant labor brigades must have been, from an economic point of view, of surpassing marginality. It tests the imagination to fathom the megalomanic minds of those who devised this monstrous scheme. The survivors sought to escape by foot as individuals or, less frequently, in small groups. Their goal was to reach the Thai border and presumed sanctuary.

The psychological act of becoming a refugee and then, from a personal rather than a legal perspective, gradually ceasing to be a refugee is dealt with in the final part of some of these essays. This process of reestablishing an identity is quite different from the adaptations undertaken by the voluntary economic migrant although there are some parallels. These factors are clearly brought out in Lucy Nguyen-Hong-Nhiem's essay. Gabrielle Tyrnauer, an anthropologist who originally came to America as a child with her parents fleeing Hitler's occupation of Austria, makes the point in an unpublished essay that one always remains a refugee in certain aspects of behavior. While assimilation implies an act of becoming, it is a process that has no fixed terminus.

These essays reflect the students' diversity. There is an important subethnic variation. Some of the students are products of mixed marriages and have multiple heritages—Sino-Vietnamese, Sino-Cambodian, and Sino-Lao. Aside from cultural diversity, there are the important variables of gender and age at departure, as well as the date of departure, which influence the ways in which the experiences are now perceived. Whether the escape and subsequent establishment in America were done with some family members or as an "unaccompanied minor" is a matter of key importance. Those students adopted by American families had a very different experience from that of the students who came with relatives.

Those who left in April 1975, immediately at the end of the war, represented the urban professional, business, managerial, and government elites. Their adaptations have been easier and more successful than many of the subsequent "boat people" who were sometimes of provincial working-class or rural peasant background. Coming from a village or even a small town to urban America is quite different from moving from Saigon of the middle 1970s.*

The student essays reflect how critical it is for individuals to experience a new country in a social framework that includes at least

*For an excellent introduction to the literature on refugees, see David Haines, ed., *Refugees in the United States: A Reference Handbook* (Westport, Conn.: Greenwood Press, 1985). This survey contains chapters on the Khmers, Lao, and Chinese from Southeast Asia and presents detailed bibliographies and a selected annotated bibliography.

some family members. In their papers all the students indicate the pervasive influence of family ideology and the need to relate their values to those of their parents even when the ties have been broken, to maintain a family tradition even without the kin network. As these students acquire formal citizenship, as many already have, their voices assume an independent legitimacy within the multicultural heritage of American society. It is to be hoped that these voices will gain greater prominence and enrich our society in the process. It can also be hoped that they will provide us with a more balanced worldview as we look east as well as west.

LUCY NGUYEN-HONG-NHIEM

Becoming a Refugee, Being a Refugee, Ceasing to Be a Refugee

AMONG the autobiographical essays written by students enrolled in the courses "Cultures of Southeast Asia" and "Vietnamese Literature," a selection is presented here in their original form. I feel proud and delighted to have had the opportunity to teach these courses and these students. I am proud not only because I am able to teach about Southeast Asian cultures—about my own culture—but also because, like my students, I am a refugee. I share their background and their traumatic experiences. We are bonded by the common knowledge that being a refugee means having lived with wars, losses, killings, and deaths. Being a refugee means having to leave everything and everyone behind, in search of a new land, a new home, a new life. It means paying a high price for freedom.

I was born in the Year of the Cat (1939). In Vietnam, years, or "ages" as they are called, go by cycles of twelve, and each age is represented by a different animal. The Vietnamese believe that the age of the cat is a particularly good one for women. A woman born under the sign of the cat will have an easy and comfortable life, like that of the cat. She will be protected and spoiled by her loved ones. Like the cat, she will be friendly, smart, quick, not aggressive but able to defend herself when attacked. This seemed to be true for me during my first cycle of twelve years. I then began the second cycle of my life, and things began to change.

In the first year of my second cycle, I was a thirteen-year-old student at a French Catholic boarding school. There I experienced an incident that marked me for the rest of my life. One of my Vietnamese classmates was talking while our French teacher was giving her lecture. The French nun pointed her finger at the student, yelling in the most contemptuous tone which I still recall vividly: "Vous, les Annamites, savez-vous ce que c'est que la politesse?" (You, Annamese, don't you know how to be polite?) The term "Annamese" in this case referred to all the people of Vietnam. At that time, when Vietnam was a French colony, the term had an extremely insulting connotation.

When the cat receives the most challenging provocation, it can no longer remain friendly. I stood up, looked right into the teacher's eyes, and said: "Sister, you take back that term "*Annamite*" and apologize to my people or we will punish you for your barbarian behavior!"

The nun responded: "You little worm, get out of here!"

I did not move. She ran to the principal who soon appeared in the classroom, pointing at me:

"For your misconduct, you will eat alone for one week, and you will have nothing but bread and water."

That was the verdict, without trial. Though I knew it to be unjust, I expected, and accepted, this punishment. However, I discovered that there was more to come; the eight academic prizes I had been awarded over the course of the school year were taken away from me. Colonized people pay a high price for freedom of speech. At the age of thirteen I had already experienced oppression, repression, and injustice.

By the age of twenty-five (the Year of the Cat again), I had graduated from the Faculty of Pedagogy at the University of Saigon. By then I was married and had two daughters and I was appointed a teacher of French in a public high school for girls. I was well aware of the contradiction between the values of the French enlightenment philosophers I had studied and the way in which I had been mistreated as a young girl in school. Perhaps that was why I had become a teacher of French myself: I would get revenge on that nun from my past by instilling ideas of liberty, equality, and justice in the minds of my own students.

A new life began. A fortune-teller stopped by my house one day and predicted that I would encounter many difficulties at the beginning of my fourth cycle of age, at the age of thirty-seven when the

Lucy Nguyen-Hong-Nhiem's family at a reunion in Kontum, central Vietnam, on New Year's Day 1972.

Year of the Cat came again. I did not pay attention to her predictions; for me, they were mere superstition. Later, experiencing the political turmoil of Vietnam, I felt those predictions being realized. On April 27, 1975, circumstances forced me to leave Vietnam. With my four children I boarded an American military plane. Left behind were my husband, my father, my sister and her ten children, my sister-in-law and her son; my two brothers were already jailed in areas under Communist control.

How could I depart without my eighty-seven-year-old father? When I asked him if he would leave with me, he answered: "The most unfortunate thing that can happen to a man is to die away from his home and his ancestors' graves. Your mother's grave is not yet covered over with green grass. How could I leave it?" My mother had passed away the year before, and he was still mourning her. Then my father cried. The first time I had seen him cry had been at my mother's funeral. This was the second and last time that that strong man let his tears out. It was so painful for me that I felt, as the Vietnamese expression says, that "my entrails were cut into pieces." I tried to comfort him: "Please do not cry, Father! I am not leaving for long—I am going overseas to continue my studies as you have always wished. I will be back soon after graduation. I promise you, it won't be long."

I knew I was lying, but to my great surprise he stopped crying and smiled. I will never forget that smile of satisfaction on his wrinkled face. I left my father and my family in tears, promising myself to fulfill my father's dream: to get an education for myself and for my children.

The hope of fulfilling his dream gave me the courage to board that plane full of women and children, which was ready to take us away from our war-torn country. The same motive pushes many of our children, particularly our young men, to leave their families, to risk their lives on the high sea in order to seek refuge in a free country where they will have access to a truly free education. However, the road from our country to the United States is a long and arduous one.

My journey to America began with the door of the airplane closing behind me, shutting me off from my own world. At that moment, my physical connection to my homeland was severed completely and absolutely. When I felt the wheels of the plane leave the ground I was shaken by strong emotions. A painful sensation of loss penetrated me: I knew I had left my family, never to see them again; I had left my country, never to return. I had become a refugee. It was at that moment that I realized I was a homeless, stateless creature at the mercy of Fate. Great fear overwhelmed me, and I started to tremble. I looked around and saw women and children weeping. My own four innocent daughters (the youngest nine, the eldest seventeen) kept asking me, "Mother, where are we going?" I could not answer because I myself did not know. All I knew was that we were in the air, flying to an unknown world. I was too numb to wonder if this world would be kind or hostile to us. The future was totally uncertain.

At our first stop at Clark Air Base in the Philippines we were well received. It seemed auspicious, thank God! After three days, we were taken to the island of Guam. Other refugees could describe the miserable conditions of the refugee camp there and the terrible weather of the island; as for myself, I did not have time to pay attention to those conditions. I was preoccupied with getting in line to obtain a visa for the United States. For two days and two nights I waited in the open air, at the mercy of the sun and rain, with no roof other than my umbrella. The second night of waiting was the longest night I have experienced in my life. Would I be given the visa that would allow me to go to the United States?

Reports I had read in Vietnam had led me to believe that were I to be refused that visa, I would end up a slave in Guam, forced to labor on behalf of American interests. Needless to say, I was terrified as I stood in that line. That night, looking up, I could see the dark blue sky and its countless stars. Looking around on earth, I saw the tents and the people crawling in and out of them like busy ants. The painful sensation of total deprivation, of family, home, village, country, invaded me again. I felt acute pain in my chest and was barely able to breathe. That torrent of emotions threatened to suffocate me physically as well as emotionally. I felt so fragile and vulnerable standing there between heaven and earth, at the whim of forces of a merciless nature. My life was like a very fine string ready to snap.

Then, the immigration officer called my name for an interview. I held my breath until he affixed his seal on my I-94 card. It was 4:00 A.M. on May 13, 1975. I could breathe again. I remembered my mother had told me that I had been born at 4:00 A.M. while she tried to reach the hospital in a small boat crossing the Dakbla River in Kontum, central Vietnam, under a dark sky full of stars, surrounded by myriads of fireflies (*lucioles* as they are called in French). Thus I was baptized "Lucia." And indeed, early that morning in May 1975 I was born again, under the starlit sky of Guam, born to a new life in the United States, one that promised not to be easy.

My first year in the United States as a refugee was one of warm consolation in spite of the bitter cold of New England. After six months of resettlement in Springfield, Massachusetts, I was accepted as a graduate student by the French department of the University of Massachusetts at Amherst. I will never forget the encouragement, the support both material and moral, and the genuine generosity of the faculty and staff members of that department. I was thrilled by the idea that I would really be able to fulfill my father's dream: that I would get as much education as possible for myself and for my children.

Those six years of graduate studies wrapped in love and care were enough to make up for past losses. But no amount of warmth during the days could keep the fear out of my nights. I used to have nightmares about my husband and my brothers, then detained in "re-education camps" in Vietnam. No matter how pleasant my days were, my nights were filled with a latent fear, fear of a sudden appearance of bad luck. I woke up every morning praying, "Oh God, may my day be peaceful without bad news from home!" But once the day started I did not have time to think or to fear. Every day was a day of struggle, the struggle to "fit in" as a refugee in the process of acculturation. But the more I struggled the more I felt I would always be an outsider. The "insiders" seemed to invite me in, but there was something, something that made me feel uncomfortable. I stayed outside, observing the "insiders," envying them. Would I ever be one of them?

Unfortunately, I was unable to put as much effort as I would have liked into trying to reach them, since so much of my energy was directed in so many different ways. For years I lived a nomad's life, moving from house to house, my belongings packed in suitcases and cartons. At first, I tried to unpack them, to put them on shelves, but by the time I finished doing so, it was time to move again. No permanent residence! My job suffered the same situation: changes from institution to institution. Is nomadism the lot reserved for displaced peoples? Being a refugee means having constant feelings of instability and insecurity. That insecurity has affected not only my physical circumstances but also my relationships with others. As a refugee, I try to avoid conflicts and confrontations with people. I no longer stand up and talk back as I did to that French nun so many years ago. I was at home then, but I am on foreign soil now.

Everything I see in this foreign land makes me think about Vietnam. The great abundance of food disturbs me; the generous care of animals makes me jealous. If my people over there could have just what is thrown in the garbage here, they would not starve. If our children over there could have one hundredth of the care and love given to dogs here, they would not have to wander on the streets "licking the few grains of rice left on the banana leaves," as the Vietnamese expression goes, referring to orphans who have no home and no food and are forced to eat whatever they can scavenge in the streets.

And so I keep myself busy. I try not to allow myself any spare time, because I am grief stricken when I think of my country and my people left behind. But I am torn: I do not want to think about Vietnam, yet I keep thinking about it. I fill my time with books about Vietnam; if I cannot go home physically, at least I make imaginary trips there. I organize cultural activities and try to re-create that familiar atmosphere of festivities, those sounds known to me since birth, hoping they will soothe the burning pains I feel inside. Those pains are pains of nostalgia for a lost homeland. Being a refugee means knowing that you will never go home.

Especially for older people, unless you know that you will find your homeland again, that one day you will go home and help rebuild your country, then you never cease to be a refugee. Being a refugee is not a status; it is a permanent state within a soul that has no permanence, living in a world of impermanence.

Tonight, sitting in my house in Amherst, under the beautiful cold moon of the first month of the Year of the Cat, I write this essay and reflect on my past while wrestling with my future. I hope that the rough years have passed and that better years are coming so that I can fulfill my Fate, that of a woman born under the auspices of the Cat, that friendly animal portending an easy and pleasant life.

Reading the students' autobiographies, one certainly can see that in spite of the many hardships and obstacles these young people have encountered, in general they seem to feel happy and satisfied with their present situations—satisfied because they are in school, because they have a chance to fulfill their dreams and the dreams of their parents to get a good education in order to build a better future for themselves, their families, and their people.

While I am pleased to see these students satisfied, I myself will not be completely satisfied, nor do I think they will be, until we are assured that their younger fellow refugees will be given the same opportunities for access to higher education. Institutions of higher learning need to be sensitive to the situations of these students. These young men and women are adjusting to a new culture along with a new educational system. Few young Southeast Asian refugees have the confidence and the courage necessary to apply to college. It is important that colleges and universities be aware that those few students who do want to go on with higher education are invaluable to their communities. There is a critical need in the refugee community for bilingual, bicultural professionals. These younger brothers and sisters of those whose stories you will read, along with their older siblings, can meet that need. If these new applicants continue to be rejected as I see happening at present, then not only is harm done to their communities but also to their desire to learn, to improve themselves, and to fulfill their mission of serving their people. Worse still, a lack of sensitivity to the Southeast Asian refugee applicants now can discourage even younger generations from considering higher education.

My own hope is that these young people understand that, in our traditions, meeting the family and community's need is a sacred mission, a way of paying back all that they have received. The students whose essays you will read here are enjoying their higher education. Having been forced out of their homelands, they must prepare themselves to serve their people. They are learning to overcome their past traumas and to apply themselves to the task at hand. I trust that their writings will allow you to gain some insight into their past experiences and move you closer to an understanding of their present situation. Perhaps you will want to work alongside them as they fulfill their mission and become a dynamic part of the constantly evolving American experience. People of the Far East who love nothing but peace have come near.

From Vietnam

DO MINH BANG

Memories from the Past

THE GOOD AND BAD OLD DAYS

IN our school system, we had to take the baccalaureate exam to graduate from high school. If we failed the baccalaureate examination, we would have to repeat the year until we passed. The examinations were on a national standard. We used to have two baccalaureate certificates, one at the end of the eleventh grade, and one at the end of the twelfth grade.

In the early 1970s, the government decided to drop the baccalaureate exam for the eleventh grade. However, our school continued a very tough curriculum for our eleventh grade in order to prepare the students for the decisive final year. Therefore, we had many more classes than in the previous years. We had to go to school in the morning and some afternoons in a week.

The year was coming along. Most of my time was spent in the classroom. We stayed in school from eight o'clock through the afternoon classes. The afternoon classes never lasted four hours, hence we had part of the afternoon for ourselves. Some would leave school and go somewhere else. A lot of us would stay until five o'clock. Sometimes we studied in the library. Sometimes we would walk around and talk, and many times, we would watch the soccer games. Whenever we had a break, we would meet together in the hallway and chat for a long time. I had found out that the older we got, the more childish we became. We argued much more that year about things that were totally immaterial.

We would laugh over nothing, like idiots. Sometimes we even chased each other through the halls like sixth graders. I felt that all the students in my class that year were trying hard to hang on to those beautiful years of high school. We were afraid of the coming year when we would feel old and miserable because of the pressure. This seemed to be the last year of high school, when all of us still had a chance to play and joke.

The year passed by with much laughter, with much chatting, chasing, blushing, and also much studying. It was again Christmastime, but this year, because of the political uncertainty, we did not have any big celebration in the school. However, in our class, we decided to organize a small party within our class on December 24. The girls did all the cooking and decorating. The guys prepared a stage and musical instruments. Chi and Thom spent a whole evening making cutouts from crepe paper. Tuong Van, Liet Xuan, and many others were running around to bring in food and drinks. When the party started, the boys said they needed another amplifier for the electric guitar, so again someone was missing and we had to wait. When the amplifier arrived, we had a blackout because the generator in the neighborhood failed. We sat in the dark and ate, but we did not talk to each other because we were so disappointed. Finally, everyone left in sadness. We had spent too much time and effort for the event to have it turn out to be wasted.

Our New Year came shortly after Christmas. That year, Henry Kissinger and Le Duc Tho were signing a peace treaty in Paris. We were told we would have an armistice on our New Year. The students discussed peace at every corner. We really did not know what to expect, though we were excited. Our teachers advised us to stay inside the house on these days, since we didn't know who was who, who would be friendly and who wouldn't be. It was sad and ironic; for many years we wanted peace so badly and now it had seemed to come, but people were very afraid and uncertain about it. Under any circumstances, our class wanted to have a celebration before saying good-bye. We were not sure then if we could come back after the New Year. "What if?" was a common question among us.

Our New Year was something distinctive. We believed anything we did at the beginning of the year would affect us for the whole year. For instance, if we worked at the beginning of the year, we would have to work all year along. If we had good luck, there would be money in the first new days (at least the first seven days of the lunar calendar). Our hopes for luck included new clothes, especially for chil-

Vietnamese classical musicians in the ancient royal capital of Hué.
Photo by Le Van Khoa.

dren, money to spend, and good food to eat. People didn't want to work, so we had to prepare food for many days in advance so that on New Year's Day we could just eat, play cards, go to the movies or the parks; in general, all wanted to have a good time.

The New Year's Days were fantastic, but the few days before New Year's were not fun for adults. All the housework and food preparation needed to be done. The work was exhausting. Every year at this time, my mother would make us paint the house, inside and outside, so that it would look new and clean. She would have all the blankets and mosquito nets in the house washed and dried. All the brass candle holders in the house had to be polished until you could see yourself in them. And, worst of all, all the china and glassware, which she never let us use for fear we would break them, also had to be washed so that they wouldn't look dusty in the cupboard.

Every year, I remember spending at least three to four hours going through those glasses and bowls. I always asked my mother why we didn't wash them during the year so that we wouldn't have to do so much cleaning at once. We did wash them during the year; however, everything had to be spotless for the New Year. There was no way around my mother. Then we had to rush to the market to shop in a huge crowd. There was food to buy and especially material for new clothes for us and my younger brothers. Children were always privileged at New Year's. Then we had to sew new clothes and prepare the food. In my house, we took turns with the work. Two people worked in the kitchen and one person prepared the clothes.

For the southerners food was the most important thing. For New Year's we would have watermelons, a lot of them, rice cakes, and fruit candies. We spent many days in the kitchen, cleaning and cutting up the fruits and then simmering them in sugar on a low heat until they dried. Finally, we had to dry them under the sun so that they would keep for a long time. The best place to dry the fruits was on the roof of the house. If we were lucky the fruit would still be there in the afternoon when it was time to take it back inside the house. If we weren't so lucky, they would somehow end up in some neighborhood kid's stomach. My mother could never figure out how the kids could climb up to her roof to take the candies. She had forgotten that she also climbed up and put the candies there in the first place. Logic never worked with my mother.

We also made pickles and prepared enough meat for seven

days. Pork was most popular. Simply, it was cheaper and more available. Chicken was planned only for the first day. My mother didn't like to have chicken for many days. My arms were sore after a day of making pickles because we had to pack them really tight, so that they could sour more quickly. Another thing we did was to tie a kilogram of mung beans in a thin, light canvas bag, hang it in a damp, dark place, and soak it in water twice a day. After about three days we would open the bag, shake off all the green shells, and then have white, delicious-looking bean sprouts. Bean sprouts were my mother's specialty, so she felt bad, sad, or happy depending on how the bean sprouts turned out. My mother had spent her whole life in the kitchen, food was her pride and also her accomplishment. Her rewards through the years were when we ate and ate. She felt happy and successful when her children finished their meals. She thought she had done a very good job. Indeed, she had. In the years since then, with the money I earned and the foods available, I have never once made a meal as good as what she made on the tightest budget. I guess it was the taste of home that my mother provided for us.

The rice cakes were traditional, as traditional as the watermelons. Yet they were much more sentimental because of the time we spent to make them. (We bought watermelons from the market.) There were two kinds of cakes we would prepare. For one, we would wrap the sweet rice around prepared mung beans and meat, squeeze everything up tightly in banana leaves, and tie them with straw. Then we would boil the cakes in water for eight hours until they were done. We would take them out and store them in the kitchen until we were ready to eat. For another kind we had to grind the sweet rice into powder, mix it with brown sugar, wrap the dough around prepared mung beans, salted or sweetened as one chose, and make it into a ball. We wrapped each ball lightly in banana leaves and bent the banana leaves in the shape of a cone. Then we would steam them. This kind cooked much faster, taking about ten to fifteen minutes of steaming. Usually, the neighbors would put money together to buy enough firewood to heat a really big caldron of water. We would each put our rice cakes into that caldron. This pooling saved everyone money, and the women in the neighborhood had a chance to sit and gossip all night long near the fire while they were guarding it. I could hardly sleep on these nights, because I always heard laughter and talking. The stories I heard were usually the wildest, ones that I would never hear on normal days. The cooking of the rice cakes itself was not so sentimental, but I guess the time spent together was.

Once a year was enough for the gathering together, because in the coming year they never stopped discussing the stories they heard that night and the people involved. It was a good time in a small society.

On the twenty-third of the last month in the old year, we had to have a simple celebration to say good-bye to the "Táo." We believed Táo was a saint sent from heaven to guard the earth. Every family would have its own Táo. This Táo always sat in the kitchen to watch what happened during the year, and so he had a black face due to the smoke from the coal used for cooking. There was also a hierarchy among these Táo, the small ones guarded families, the big ones guarded villages and towns. Táo would have to go back to heaven to report to God on the twenty-third of the last month and would be back down to earth on the last day for the coming year. My mother would say good-bye to Táo by burning one stick of incense with a small plate of homemade fruit candies and a small glass of water so that he wouldn't be hungry or thirsty on the way. I didn't know if he was hungry or thirsty on the way back to heaven or not, because right after the stick of incense burned down, my mother always distributed the candies among her children. We knew that, so every year we would wait outside the kitchen to ask "is he gone yet?" so that we could have our treat. On the last day of the year, the children were allowed to stay up late. Sometimes we were even allowed to stay up all night until the New Year if we wanted to. At midnight my family would burn block after block of firecrackers to chase away the bad spirits of the old year and welcome the good spirits of the new year. Most of the time, I would go to bed before midnight and ask my mother to wake me in time for the firecrackers. It was fun because everyone everywhere was setting off firecrackers. The continuous popping sounds and the red papers of the crackers flying all over the place marked a joyful time in my childhood.

In my early years, I remembered what a good time I had at New Year. My mother used to stack the whole attic with watermelons, we had two dozen big rice cakes, and we wouldn't finish the cone rice cakes until a month and a half later. That was the golden time! It gradually disappeared as the years went by. People got poorer and poorer, or at least we did. In our family the New Year's new clothes were omitted for the older children. Only the younger ones still had their treats, but it was hard for my mother. The work load remained the same with washing and cleaning. We didn't repaint the house for lack of money. We didn't need to polish the candle holders anymore, since they were long gone to the black market, probably to pay for a few months of our school fees. The glassware remained so that my mother could give them to my brothers when they got married as an inheritance, for she had no jewelry to pass on. The only decent piece of jewelry she had left was her watch, which she had to mortgage in a jewelry store so that she could buy two watermelons and two rice cakes to keep up with the tradition. My mother no longer had to worry that the children in the neighborhood would eat up her fruit candies because we didn't make any; we couldn't afford to.

It was the last day of the old year. The next day, at eight o'clock, the first day of our New Year, the war would stop. At night, while waiting for New Year's Eve, Vinh, my younger brother, sat next to me. He was cutting his fingernails. My sister teased him:

"No wonder tomorrow we will have peace. He is cutting his nails, for once in a thousand years."

All of us cracked up. When my sister disappeared into the kitchen, Vinh let out a long breath:

"It's so exciting!" he said, grinning. "Tomorrow, we will no longer have the war. I wonder what it's like to have peace."

"I don't know." I answered, "We've never had peace since I was born."

It was eight o'clock on the first day of New Year. We were supposed to have peace then, but the artillery in the nearby village was shaking our house. Soon we heard the planes at the Tan Son Nhut airport taking off. This was not very far from our house. We all jumped out of bed and went down on the floor. In case of artillery, we would have to climb under my parents' bed to avoid the debris. Vinh was grinning with me, half awake: "There goes our peace!"

My mother was crying bitterly in the kitchen: "Oh God! It came so close. I thought my sons could come home."

There went our peace, as Vinh said, and also there went our New Year. I took heed of the advice and stayed home all the time so that in case of tragedy, we would be a whole family together. We did not observe any customs that year. We did not go to temple either. That was one of the customs, which we had kept for years.

We went back to school. We did not even mention the peace we were to have. We totally ignored it so that our lives wouldn't have to change. But yet, as we were trying hard to forget it, we couldn't help being sad for the broken promises.

The school year went on with normal classes, school work, and examinations. It was surprising that we did not behave childishly any more in this second half of the year. We became very severe and studied very hard. We did not watch the soccer games any longer. We also walked around the school less frequently than before. The library was more crowded. More and more people preferred to stay inside. What went wrong, no one knew. It was just a change of the season I guessed; we began the season of the adults!

A GOOD FRIEND

It was again a rainy day. I had just finished the last book in my collection that night. I was going to downtown Saigon to buy a few more. My father was ready to leave the house, and my sister was planning a trip downtown herself. My sister and I decided to stick around my father on the trip so that he would pay the bus fare, and we would be able to save a few piasters for ourselves. The three of us walked to the end of the street to get to the station. The three-wheeled pickup trucks with two long benches along the side were used in this area for transportation instead of buses. We called them "Lambretta." Inside Saigon, there were both buses and Lambrettas, but many people used these trucks because they did not have any schedule. Every truck could carry ten people at most, and as soon as the truck was full, it would depart. These trucks ran more frequently than the buses, and they were also more dangerous.

The Lambretta took us downtown. My father got off in front of Tao-Dan Garden, a park in Saigon. My sister and I continued downtown. My sister was looking for shoes, and I was heading for the bookstore.

Saigon was always crowded, too crowded! Even the bookstore was full of people. At every corner of the bookstore, I would find somebody around me while I was trying to select a book. Eventually, the crowd made me tired and nervous, so I decided to get out of the mess. I did not want to go home so soon, so I decided to go to visit a friend since Saigon was halfway between my house and hers.

Lai had been my closest friend since early childhood. We were friends from third until fifth grade. Our high school started at sixth grade. We had to split up then because of different family backgrounds. We both failed the entrance examination to enter public school. We had to attend private schools. I went to one high school in central Saigon, which my older brother was then attending. My friend went to a Buddhist school in Cholon with a mutual friend. It was much closer to her house. I transferred to my present school when my parents moved to the outskirts two years later.

Her name, Lai, meant "mixed." Her mother married a Frenchman. After her father went back to France, her mother worked very hard to raise her. The house was very poor, at the end of a small street. Not even a motorcycle could get in. We could not ride a bike on that path. We had to push it. The house was four meters square. It consisted of a ground floor and an attic. Her family resided on the ground floor and rented the attic to a friend. In the old times, I would go to school a little early so that I could stop by and walk to school with her. After she got to know Lai my mother would sometimes allow me to go quite early to her house. Then we would sneak up to the attic while her friend was at work. We lay on the wooden floor of the attic and felt "snobbish" as if we were on the second floor of a big mansion. I guessed that being at a high altitude made us feel very important. That was many years ago. Now and then, even though I had moved far away from the city, I still found time to come back to visit her, and we would still climb up to the attic and sit and talk for many hours. We still felt important, no longer because the high altitude made us feel like we were in a big mansion, but because we had each other. What we talked about changed from year to year, from school work to poetry, from dream to adventure, from religion to society, and even from romance to reality. Sometimes we read to each other the poems we wrote, or she would show me her drawings and I would read her my short stories.

It was peaceful until that year. She married after New Year. It was an arranged marriage. We had talked so much about many things but not once about love, until the day she married. She was crying and told me about her romance. She had loved the boy next door, but she did not dare tell her mother. And she could not refuse to marry the man she had never met. Her mother had arranged with an old friend to have her son marry Lai. This old friend was very rich. She owned a retail store for tires in Cholon. Lai's mother wanted her to have a good life, since her own life was so hard. I still remember very well how I suffered for her on her wedding day as she walked from her house to the car with her new husband. The boy next door was watching from his window.

There was nobody in the house, except her younger brother. He told me that she was at her mother-in-law's house. Once more, I hopped on the wheeled truck and entered the Chinatown of Saigon, Cholon.

I found the house with difficulty. I had been there only once, on her wedding day. It was a big house with a tall fence in front. Inside the fence, tires were piled up to the ceiling. The front door seemed tiny behind the gigantic pile of rubber.

I hesitated for a long time before I rang the bell. I was very nervous all of a sudden. She appeared behind the door, and as she saw me, she ran quickly outside, opened the gate, and pulled me in. She quietly dragged me all the way from the front gate through a very long house, to the kitchen. We then sat on stools, near the stove. I took a long breath, looked at her with wonder. She understood my look, she whispered:

"My mother-in-law does not want me to have friends. I don't dare to talk with you in the living room. It's better if we stay here."

I shook my head, trying to make sure that I was awake, then I sighed:

"That's all right, Lai. You don't have to apologize. I am very happy to see you. So, how are you doing?"

"I am doing fine," she said. Then she asked me how my school had been. I told her about my friends and the past school year. For some reason, I left "Brown Eyes" out of the conversation. I did not want to remind her anything at all about the romance we used to have at that age. I was afraid to cause her pain since she was walking away from all of this, trying hard to forget all the fun that we were supposed to have at the age of sixteen.

"I miss school," she said. "You are the first one of my friends to come visit me after my wedding."

I tried to keep her from the memory of old times:

"Well, did you have a honeymoon?" I asked.

"Yes, we went to Vung-Tau, stayed there for a week. Would you like to see the pictures?"

"Of course," I said. She took out the album and showed me the pictures of her wedding and her honeymoon. I was amazed to see how beautiful she looked in the Western dresses. I commented:

"You looked just like a movie star in these pictures."

She smiled, showed me one of her best pictures. The dress she wore was stunning. I suggested:

"Why don't you show me this dress, I'd like to see how you would look in it for real."

"Well, I don't have the dress anymore. My mother-in-law rented them for me for the two weeks of our honeymoon. She returned them a long time ago," she said with half a smile.

I just didn't know what else to say in such a situation. Finally, I changed the subject so that I could hide my sad eyes:

"Do you go home often?"

"I go home once every two months," she answered.

"That's good. I did not meet your mother, only your younger brother was home when I stopped by. How is she? Is she still selling chickens at the bus station?"

Lai put her hand on her chin to support her head as she leaned on the round table:

"She is fine," she said, "and she is still selling chickens at the bus station. I work here for my mother-in-law. I wash the tires as they come in from shipment. My mother-in-law gives me five thousand piasters a month for allowance." She took a deep breath and continued:

"I save a lot of it, and bring it home for my mother when I come home."

"She must be happy," I smiled.

"Yes, very," she said, and then she smiled. "At least I could help her out a little. My younger brother never cares about her."

"He will, he is still too young. Give him a few years."

"Am I not too young?" she asked.

I burst into tears, embraced her, and felt my heart ache. I felt her tears on my shoulders. She pushed me away and said: "Why are we crying like two little kids?"

"Because we are not strong enough," I answered.

The sentence sounded so funny even though it was meant to be sad that it made both of us laugh. The tears were still on our cheeks but we were cracking up like two cheerful little children. We laughed as children and we cried as children, like she said. What were we if we were not children then?

The laughing soon came to a stop. I felt very sad again. She lowered her head and whispered: "I think you should go home. If you go now, you will get home before dark."

I looked at her silently, but there were a thousand things

running through my head. Then, I had to agree with her: "Yes, I think so. I'll have to change the bus in Saigon again. I hate it."

I picked up my hat. We walked quietly to the gate. "I'll see you again sometime, maybe at New Year," I said when we reached the gate. We embraced each other once more. This time I pushed her away, but kept her hand in mine. I gave her a firm squeeze before I walked away. I did not turn my head, but I knew she was standing there. I walked to the corner as fast as I could so that I wouldn't keep her at the gate any longer. When the Lambretta arrived I jumped into my seat quickly. I did not look back to see whether she was still standing there when the truck passed by her house.

TA MINH TRI

Memories

EVERYONE has a few memories in life, especially from when he was young. Personally, I think that the happiest and nicest time in my life was from when I was five years old until I was sixteen. At that time, I was an innocent child, my mind was full of joy and fun, without worries about everyday realities such as shelter, money, and food.

I remember the first time I went to school. On that morning, my mother woke me up, cooked breakfast for me, and took me to school. On the way to school the weather was cool, which made me feel comfortable. While we were walking along the road, my mother said: "My son, there is your school. Do you see it?" I said: "Yes, Mother, I do." I had seen my school many times before when she had carried me to go shopping, but at that time it looked a little strange to me as I gazed at it. Coming closer, I saw a large green gate with rust where the paint had been chipped off. Looking through the gate, the school took up about 600 square feet, including a backyard, four classrooms, and a principal's office. My mother took me to the principal's office to meet Mrs. Thu, my first teacher.

Although she looked very friendly, after my mother left me alone with Mrs. Thu, I started to cry. I was wishing I could go back to my mother. My teacher gave me some candies and some toys to play with. A few hours later I started making friends with other children in my class. A few days later, I began to love school. Every morning I woke up by myself, had breakfast, and ran as fast as a rabbit to school because

Ta Minh Tri (center) and classmates celebrate the Vietnamese New Year (Campus Center, University of Massachusetts, Amherst). Photo by Steve Long.

I was learning how to draw some easy objects such as suns, trees, and squares.

I cannot remember how long it took me to go from being a nervous, shy boy to being a more relaxed, bold, and confident person who enjoyed learning at school.

Time passed by, summer came, school closed, and vacation started. For the first couple of days of summer I was bored, missing my teacher and my classmates. I was so lonely that my mother took me to Sa Dec, a country town located about forty miles south of Saigon, to visit my favorite grandmother who always gave me candies and toys whenever I asked for them. My grandmother loved me because I was her first grandchild and she asked my Uncle Tam to take me fishing every afternoon and swimming on the hot days in summer. More than that, he took me to the river, rowing a small boat to catch the fish, or we went into the forest to hunt rabbits. One day, while Uncle Tam and I were fishing, he asked me, "Tri, how is your father? I have not seen him for the last two years." I said, "I also have not seen him often but he looked fine about three months ago, which was the last time I saw him."

Although my father was Chinese, he spoke Vietnamese well and was able to understand Vietnamese songs. He was a businessman. He often went overseas for his business; therefore he did not have many opportunities to get to know my brothers and me.

I remember that one summer, unlike other summers, instead of going to see grandmother, my father took me to visit my grandfather in Hong Kong, where they were speaking Chinese. My grandfather was really disappointed with us because my father had not taught me to speak Chinese, so my grandfather and I were unable to communicate. Because of that problem, our trip was not as much fun as the trips I used to make to see my grandmother.

When we got back to Vietnam, my father started to teach my brothers and me Chinese by talking to us, but we did not learn much because my father had to leave home for his business. He did not have much time to spend with us. Six months later, my grandfather decided to live in Vietnam for two years. During that time my life changed. Normally, I went out with other children in my neighborhood to play soccer or basketball after school, and came back at dinner time, and studied at night. Now I had to stay with my grandfather to learn Chinese. After a while I could understand his Chinese and began to love him.

In 1972, I was twelve years old. The war became more and more serious; my grandfather could not stay any longer in Vietnam. He had to leave and wanted to take me back to Hong Kong with him, but my parents wished to keep me with them. After he left, my father decided to do his business in Vietnam. Although he made less money than before, he felt happy to have more time to spend with us and get to understand us better.

The war from 1972 to 1975 affected the country greatly, but because we lived in Saigon my family was not touched. The presence of my father at home brought our family warmth and happiness. Especially at dinner time, my father talked a lot about his life and his business, and he tried to teach us what he knew, which he had never had many opportunities to do previously.

In 1975, the Communist party from North Vietnam took over South Vietnam. I was fifteen years old, old enough to see and understand what the Communists would do to our people. I was bored at school, especially in political classes, which were required under the new government. Three years later, I finished high school and had no idea what I would do in the future. In addition, I was drafted into the Communist army shortly after I finished high school. My parents were shocked when they heard that news.

Two days before the date on which I had to start service in the army, my parents found a way for me to escape from Vietnam by boat. I remember the last day, when my parents came to see me off. My mother just said nothing. She was crying and I also remember the sadness of my father and he said with his sad and deep voice, "My son, I have to leave you now, I wish you luck and you take good care of yourself. We will try to visit you." I said nothing to my father and gave my mother a very, very deep hug before I left.

These wonderful moments are gone, but their memory will remain forever.

TRAN THI SANH

"We Are Killing Our Own Brothers, Our Souls"

My village lies about four miles northeast of the central Vietnamese city of Nha Trang. It is in the lowlands between the mountains and sea of the Ninh Hoa district, in the former Khanh Hoa Province. The village area extends about five square miles and includes extensive rice fields in the eastern section.

The villagers are all native Vietnamese. Water buffalos are among many of the villagers' most precious possessions. When water buffalos are not needed in the fields, young boys herd them. When peasants need to plant seeds, their buffalos pull plows for hours through the mud. Sometimes peasants make up songs and sing as they plow:

Oh buffalo, dear buffalo
Are you tired, dear buffalo?
I will go with you, dear buffalo
I will go with you, dear buffalo.

This is where I lived when I was a child, yet not too many people know about it. During my childhood this village had only an elementary school; it had no high school, so after I finished elementary school, I went to live with my brother in the city in order to study. It is only two miles from the district to the village, but the people who lived in town were very different from the people who lived in the village. For instance, the townspeople would compete with each other while the villagers would share. Maybe this was one of the reasons why my father chose to live in the village for his entire life.

When I was twelve years old, I lived both in the city and in the countryside. I was very close to my father. I learned from his habits and his ideas. He liked to read books and he wrote in a journal every day.

My mother, who took care of the home, was a very good wife, yet my father was an unhappy person. Nothing would satisfy him. He did not agree with either the southern or the northern governments. I still remember what he said about the Vietnamese War: "This is a crazy war; we are killing our own brothers, we are killing our souls, we are actors and victims of two powerful countries." He died of cancer in 1972. We were very sad at that time. I was a high school student. My eldest brother found all of my father's journals, short stories, longer stories, and poems. Some of them were finished but most of them lacked endings. He wrote all his feelings in his journal. I will never forget one part of his journal. "I only know how to teach my children with love. I have not yet learned which way to teach my children. My ideas do not agree with the time in which I am living."

He also wrote: "What should I do for my people? They push each other because they are hungry and they have many children to feed. The children follow the Americans and ask for money because they are poor, many girls end up in the hands of tired strangers, they sell their bodies because they want to live. They do not care for the future. . . . Do you see dancing clubs, bars, and crazy music? Many customers try to laugh because they are afraid they will cry; their soul will be deserted and bitter. . . ." My eldest brother and my mother decided to destroy all of my father's writings a few months after he died because of the tension between North and South Vietnam. Anyone with different ideas was often thrown in prison.

Day by day the Vietnamese War dragged on. We did not know when it would end. I witnessed many terrible things in my town. Mines exploded every morning, and cannons blasted every night. The people became immune to the fighting. The sounds of cannons became like background music to them.

In 1973, I visited my mother in the village only in the daytime because during the night the South Vietnamese government could not protect the villages. Only married women, old men, and children were safe in the villages at night because the North Vietnamese

Floral offerings for a Lao holiday ritual.
Photo by Sam Pettengill.

would enter the villages then looking for medicine and would capture young South Vietnamese men and women.

A few years later, in 1975, the war ended. This greatly changed my mother's village. First of all the sounds of cannons were no longer heard. Also, the population in that village increased because many young men returned from the army, and many families came back from the city. Some of them looked very happy, but most of them looked worried. The school reopened but under new organization. There was much disorder with both new people and old people. Many smiles and many tears. I started to study again after a few months of disorder. I prepared to take an important exam in order to finish high school and get a diploma. Then I took a competitive exam along with about 500 other students before entering the school of education. I began to study communism and I enjoyed Karl Marx's and Lenin's theories. I still remember the voice of my professor. It was so attractive that it made all the students listen. He was teaching this theory as a religion: equal life, no rich, no poor, no hungry, no maids, everyone shares. All of my professors were very close to us. Their lives were so simple and they were so kind. We greatly enjoyed school. As a twenty-year-old student a wonderful life presented itself. I planned to work hard for my people. Sometimes I would say to myself, "Dad was unhappy because he could not find the right way for him, but I found it." Then I finished school and I got a job in a small district. I was a very young high school teacher for that area. The idealized picture in my mind was very different from real life. I saw many hungry and homeless people. I was confused. The economy was failing. People worked very hard, but they did not get enough food to eat nor enough clothes to wear. I went to visit a few of my students' families. Most of their situations were sad. Many families had to start new lives on farms or in the mountains.

I thought a lot about communism, and what it means. I tried to be open-minded. I tried to accept it. I understood some of the reasons behind the Communists' actions, but I could not accept all of their ways. They liked to strengthen the military more than the society. I do not agree with limiting basic freedoms such as speaking, traveling, learning. I would like to be able to be an observer to watch them play the game, to compare and learn. I do not like the expansion of the Communists. I thought the red water of communism never stops. It will flow to many countries. How can we stop them? I could not find the answer. I was so confused. I could not find the way for myself. I did not know how to teach my students. I did not want to portray a picture in my students' minds without any solution. I did not like to be a liar in the lecture class. . . .

Then finally I decided to escape. I knew that for the Communists the small protest of a single person is the same as a drop of water on the ocean, but I hope that at least I made others question: "Why did they escape communism?"

PHAN HUU THANH

Not Too Young to Understand Communism

I was born in a poor family, in a far countryside. My parents were hard-working, ingenuous farmers. When I was two years old, my parents wanted to look for a better life so they decided to move to Saigon. With hard work, my parents succeeded in their business in the first years. At the beginning of our stay in Saigon, with pockets almost empty, my parents bought a small house. This happened when I was six and started my schooling.

Like other children, beside studying and playing, I did not pay attention to the outside society or to the ups and downs of my family's life. When I entered high school, my parents opened a fabric and sewing store. Because the financial situation of my family became better, my everyday life improved. Time went by until I was seventeen years old. It was 1975, when the "Civil War" between the north and south of Vietnam reached a climax. It was the time when the Communists from the north were about to take over the south. I was called to join the army of South Vietnam in February and was ordered to report in July. Tragically, South Vietnam fell into the Communist hands in April 1975.

As a young boy, I was indifferent to political events, even to the biggest events which resulted in the disappearance of a country from the world's map. I was not shocked when the Communists took over my homeland. At that time, I was mistaken in thinking that the differences between the two regimes would not harm me. Living under communism, I realized that everybody's life was controlled completely by the Communists and that people were expected to become Communists. I remember when I was a college freshman in 1978. I had to talk and act like a Communist. Otherwise, I would be considered bad and would be kicked out of school. I was told to join the Communist Youth party many times. I always thought of my future as a feeble one. I would never have a chance to follow my ideals. Hating the regime, hating the situation, I quit school and went to work.

At that time my parents' fabric and sewing goods store was closed because there were not as many customers as before. Perhaps people no longer cared about their appearance. People just hoped to have enough food for everyday survival. My parents had to change their business and they worked harder. After I quit school, I worked for a soy sauce factory that formerly belonged to my cousin but that was now controlled by the government. Not too long after I went to work, I was forced to join the Communist army. My parents were very upset about this, especially when they thought of my cousin who had been in the same situation as I was now and who was forced to join the Communist army. He fought and then died in Cambodia as a soldier.

My parents decided to prevent me from joining. They tried to convince me to leave Vietnam, and in the meantime, tried to find a way for me to escape. I disagreed because I knew that I would be far away from my family forever. I moved far away from my home to live with a cousin in the countryside because I would be arrested if I stayed home.

In 1980 I changed my mind and decided to leave Vietnam. My parents found an organization designed to help people leave the country. This group was organized by some officials of the former government in the south. They received very bad treatment after 1975. The Communists forced them into concentration camps for the purpose of brainwashing. After many years of being held, they were released and forced to live in the "New Economic Zones," which were in the wild and primitive jungles far away from civilization. Upon being put into such a situation, these people wanted to resist, but they could do nothing, so the idea of escaping communism and finding freedom in another country appealed to them. This was the only thing they could do, and they began to carry out the idea.

However, at first they had a lot of problems. One was financial. The amount of money they had altogether was not enough, so they had to look for companions. I was one of three people who responded. As my contribution I gave them two pieces of gold. The financial problem was finally solved. We now had money in hand. The next step was to buy a boat. Someone had to go to the fishing areas to seek information about this business. This work was not easy since in some areas like fishing and manufacturing, private business was no longer permitted. The Communist government tightly controlled everything. We tried and failed many times; however, at last we obtained a small boat from some fishermen who also wanted to leave the country due to Communist persecution. The boat was small, about 15 meters long and 2.5 meters wide, and was not in good condition for a long trip. We quickly rebuilt it. Some parts were replaced, and the boat was ready at last.

As a part of the preparation for the trip, we had ten days to buy food and gasoline. We bought rice and various canned foods. We did not forget to prepare a large amount of water. Also, we bought a compass, which would help us go in the right direction. Of great concern was a place to moor the boat and how to get people into it. The boat would never depart if we did not offer twenty pieces of gold to a high official in the local area. However, before departure the boat was searched and kept two days at a police post.

The boat sailed to the sea at dawn on October 25, 1980. With the help of a map and the compass, we were on our way to Singapore. Thinking about the promised land, we all were happy. We wished to see a ship from West Germany or England or the United States, because it would help make our trip shorter. Some people started to be seasick. They vomited. Some girls did the cooking and food was distributed sparingly. Night came, but nobody could sleep. The ocean looked dangerous in the dark.

A day went by and the second day began. At 10 A.M. we saw a ship. We did not know which country it was from because it was far away. To make a signal, we burned some clothing, hoping it would attract help. People yelled at the ship, but nothing worked. The ship kept its direction and disappeared on the horizon. The people became silent once again. In the evening, our captain was the first one to see a boat approaching. People were perky and started talking. The coming boat was from Singapore, where we wanted to go. It was big, about forty meters in length, five meters in width. We saw just six people on the boat. It came within twenty meters of us. Two people used a small canoe to come to talk. They spoke Chinese. Luckily, there were some Chinese-Vietnamese people on our boat. When we asked them to take us to land, they said that they could not do that since the situation was politically related; however, they would pull our boat toward a beach provided we paid them fifteen pieces of gold. We did not have that much gold because most of it had gone in the preparation. Before leaving, they gave us some water, noodles, and two cartons of cigarettes. Also, they told us the direction to get to the island nearest our position. Someone got sick as another day went by.

I felt terrible when I remembered a story about boat people who were three weeks on the sea without food and water. Their boat was without gasoline. It went in no direction while people were dying. As for us, the boat was on its third day. People were very tired, except for the fishermen and people who were in the navy before. The captain always encouraged people. He said that without storms, pirates, or something wrong with the engine, we would get to Singapore within three more days. He paid attention to sick people and gave them medicine. Also, he did not forget to remind people to stay calm in any situation.

People in our situation fear the natural environment. In the evening, the sky was cloudy. It was the beginning of a storm. People were even more afraid, but we still hoped that the storm would be light. Once again we did not get our wish. It was a big storm, lasting more than twelve hours. It began at 9 P.M. and ended at 9:30 A.M. the next morning. The small boat had to fight with huge waves. It went up and down and seemed like it would capsize at any moment. The captain and fishermen were calm. Not only were they keeping us composed, but they also had to work at keeping the boat balanced. Aside from the sound of water beating on the sides of the boat, I heard prayers from many people. We stood at the threshold of death. Some water started to get in the boat through gaps made as waves beat over it breaking down the caulking that held the wood together. A fisherman went down to check and reported that the gaps were not dangerous. The skills of the captain and fishermen were wonderful. They did not let the boat "fail" in the face of the huge waves. The boat kept going slowly in the storm.

The sky returned to its beauty as the black clouds departed. Thank God, we were still alive. As if coming back from death, we were happy and started talking. Some men volunteered to do the cooking while some others made fun of girls who had been so scared during the storm the night before. It was the first time on the trip that I saw people laugh. I tried to sleep to pass another day.

We started the fifth day with an engine problem. Smoke came out of the smokestack in circular shapes. Someone said that the engine was about to stop. To relax the people, the captain said it would be all right if we turned off the engine for a while. (We thought that without a working engine the boat would be capsized if it met another storm. This was a terrible thought.) About 10 A.M., someone woke up the others when he first saw a helicopter coming. One can imagine how happy we were. With newly found energy, everybody waved and yelled at the helicopter. A woman was crying. Perhaps she was so happy because she knew that the coming helicopter was from the United States. The captain reminded people to stay calm again. He then tried to communicate with the pilots, but the helicopter just flew around and around and finally flew away. Some people felt bad, but the captain said "The Americans would never go away when they know we are in a situation like this. They will come back." He was right. Another helicopter and a warship came toward us. The captain told us that the ship and the helicopters belonged to the Seventh Fleet of the U.S. Navy, which was on mission in the Pacific Ocean. The warship came closer and closer. We could see soldiers in uniforms. They waved at us as they saw us waving at them. Many other soldiers came out. No action was taken for twenty minutes. (I knew later that the ship was waiting for an order from its headquarters, telling them what to do with us.) At last, the ship started rescuing us. Some soldiers were ordered to do the job. One of them, with one hand on the cable, used the other hand to pull each of us up to the ship while other soldiers got ready to help if someone fell into the sea. Person after person, finally all of us, got on the ship safely. We were so happy that we seemed to forget tiredness. We talked about the storm, the boat from Singapore, and everything that had happened. We all agreed that this was the luckiest thing that happened in our lives. Someone noticed an interesting thing when we were rescued: around the ship, in the distance, there were four other U.S. warships. They went away as we left our boat behind. The warship's captain ordered it to fire at our boat. We felt a loss as we saw the sinking boat.

A doctor came to take care of us. He passed out different kinds of medicines for the skin, and directed us on their use. He especially paid attention to sick people. After taking a shower, everybody felt better. We looked funny in oversized T-shirts, jeans, and navy uniforms. Later we took turns in going to the cafeteria for food while some soldiers prepared a place for us to sleep at night. We were on the way to Subic Bay, a U.S. Navy base in the Philippines. We arrived at Subic Bay two days later and stayed there for three days. We were then transferred to Manila by bus. After a week, we were once again transferred by plane to Palawan, a big island in the Philippines where there was a refugee camp.

In the camp, I did not have to do anything but study English. I often felt lonely and homesick. I missed my mother whose whole life was lived for her children. She never seemed tired of working hard. She often said to the children "I'm working for you, for your future. To make me happy, just try to study hard, just try to be useful." Before I left the country, she repeated it, but in another way, another emotion. She said "Be a good person in your new country, and study as much as you can. You've had no chances here, so don't miss your chances there. We'll be happy with your success. Write home often." I promised her, and she cried. I had never seen her cry before. I also missed my father, my brothers and sisters. However, I felt more independent, more self-confident, and stronger than ever.

After nine months of living in the camp, I left for the United States under the sponsorship of the International Rescue Committee. In July 1981, I was resettled in Boston, Massachusetts. The first months were a time of struggle. I faced so many problems, especially the language problem. I cannot forget the day I was beaten by some American teenagers. The scars are still on my hands, in front of my eyes. Every time I look at them, I see a group of young men standing at a corner. My sixth sense told me that something bad was about to happen. I passed the street and started to go faster, hoping nothing would happen, but the young men passed the street and chased after me. I ran and fell. One guy hit my back with a baseball bat as I stood up. Some others punched me. They left when a car stopped at the scene. I felt very bad and was sick for two days. Also, I lost my new watch.

I applied for admission to a high school. Although I was a college freshman in my country, I applied for the eleventh grade. I knew that the language problem would hinder me a lot. My new life began with disappointments; however, when I thought of my parents, of their sacrifice, I felt stronger. I tried to study harder and harder and hoped that my success in school would make my family happy. I got on many

Between two cultures.
Photo by Steve Long.

honor rolls in my two years in high school. Then I received the Boston Teachers' Union scholarship and the Franklin Medal on my graduation day. I was accepted by three universities: Northeastern University, Wentworth Institute of Technology, and the University of Massachusetts. Because of financial problems, I decided to go to UMass, a state university. I also decided to live in a dormitory because I thought that my studies would not be affected by my surroundings as much.

Until now, I have done nothing but study in my second country. I hope that I will get a good job in the future and become useful to society. One thing which is encouraging is that my family is very happy with what I am doing so far here in the United States.

I promised myself to do the best I can.

NGUYEN HUNG ANH

Hopes of a Better Life

I was born in Vietnam, a poor little country that was constantly at war. My people have been living desperately and painfully under the control of many powerful countries: China, France, Japan, the United States, and Russia. I grew up at a time in which Vietnam was being torn apart and killings were happening every day and night. Then one early fall day in 1960, I, a little six-year-old boy with skipping feet, followed my mother to an elementary school, Quoc-Hoc, in Hue. The walk was long enough to raise an excited and strange feeling in my heart. In a new suit I felt very shy when all the other children in class turned and stared at me. That very first day of school meant a lot to me.

My teacher was not as mean as I had been told. He did not beat me up or make me stay after class or put me in an empty closet. I started to like him and thought that I certainly would study hard, as my mother had asked. I knew I would have a lot of presents if I did well in school, as I had my mother's promise. Then I got to know some friends who were also my neighbors, a boy, Heo, and a girl, Meo. Having two friends to go to school with every day made life beautiful. We had little to think about, but a lot to live for. My childhood at that time continued to pass filled with joy, games, and abundant food. We roamed the hills, ran along the beaches, and swam in the lakes. Meo and I were together from elementary school all the way through high school. We were very close to each other. We had nothing to hide from each other. The relationship between us was beautiful.

Unfortunately, the summer of our sophomore year, Meo went to visit her grandmother, who lived on a small farm south of Saigon. She was caught by the Communist underground and killed because they knew that her father was a member of the secret police of the Republic of South Vietnam. The death of Meo affected me so much that I did not feel like doing anything anymore.

That was not all. A couple of years later, my father was kidnapped on his way from our house to his office. The next thing we knew, the Communists had blown his head off because they condemned him for being chief judge of the city of Hue. He was then fifty. My mother was so depressed that she wished she could die with my father. My uncles had to spend a lot of time comforting her, telling her that she still had her children to take care of. Time went by, the northern Communists tried to kill many innocent people both in villages and in the cities. Every day reports of deaths and kidnappings were heard, especially on New Year's Eve in 1968, during the Tet offensive when Communists bombed a city near the border, killing thousands of people. They intended to kill all of those who were only suspected of being enemies rather than miss one of their real enemies.

The war was getting worse. No one was secure, no place was safe. We had to make a little underground basement to hide in every time the Communists bombed. It upset me so much that once I was going to quit school to join the army to help stop this tragedy, but my mother did not want me to leave school. Also, she did not want me to kill anyone. She just wanted me to be away from that crazy war and study and learn to love school as she had, as a principal of Dong Khanh High School. I obeyed her and continued going to school until South Vietnam fell under the control of the Communists.

Under the Communist government they fired my mother since my family was considered to be connected with the old government through my father's job. My brothers and I were not allowed to go to school. This happened to most of the families in South Vietnam who had been associated with the former government. Living under the new government, we lost all of our rights, even the freedom to visit relatives and friends, since the regime thought we might try to set up a party against them. People had to live together in certain places to be kept track of and had to work for the Communist party. Everyone was treated as a machine. No one was allowed to think in his or her own way. The Communists made people listen only to them and do as they were told.

They did not seem to care about the lives of the people. I therefore decided to escape from Vietnam after a few years of living under this government. My plan failed several times, and I was caught and some of my friends were killed trying to escape. Finally, one evening, the saddest evening in my life, I left the country on a little boat with sixty-five others. As the boat went out to sea, I turned back and tried to see my homeland for the last time. Mixed feelings arose in me. I thought of my mother, my brothers and sisters, my relatives, and all of my friends, who, unfortunately, still remained there.

After two days on the ocean, the engine in the boat broke at the same time as a heavy storm came. The wind was very hard and blew the boat off course. We spent two weeks without enough food and fuel. We lived through hopelessness and death. Several people died because of hunger. We had only one cup of tap water every day. But that was not all. Then came the Thai sea pirates. They took all our money and belongings. Some people tried to prevent them and were killed. Finally, we landed in the Philippines and were helped by the Pilipinos. They took care of the sick and provided us with food and shelter. We were then moved to a refugee camp. For six months in the camp I lived in peace and happiness, even though the living standards were not very high. At least, in my mind, there was hope for a brighter future. Still I knew I couldn't get in contact with my family in Vietnam.

At the end of 1981 I came to the United States. For the first time, I saw a big city under snow—Boston. It was beautiful yet too cold. I did not think I could stay here, in Massachusetts, for long, because of the cold weather. It took me over a year to get used to it. In this big city everything seemed so strange that the feeling of the first day in school came back to me as if I were still a little boy.

The first year in the United States was quite an experience for someone like me who didn't speak English. All I could say to everyone's questions was "I don't know." I felt awful and decided to go to the English Language Center where they taught English to foreigners. At that time, I was fixing broken televisions and cassette recorders. I saved some extra money, which I used to buy medicines to send back to my family in Vietnam. The next fall I applied to the University of Massachusetts at Amherst to study electrical engineering. Most of my tuition was paid by the federal government and the Commonwealth of Massachusetts. After school I worked part time to have some extra income for spending.

My mother was very pleased about my accomplishments and was proud of me. I myself did not feel too happy about being alone here when all of my family and relatives and friends were still in Vietnam. I could only think that I would use my time and energy to work myself up and achieve a better standard of living in order to help my family and others.

NGUYEN VAN NHAN

An Image of Home

I was born and grew up in a small village of about thirty houses. This village was in a mountain valley, part of a chain of mountains facing the sea. The village was divided into many parts by small streams which flowed into a large river. My hamlet was a small place compared to the other hamlets of the village. Here there were three houses, some farmland, and many fruit and shade trees. It was the most distant part of the village and close to the foot of a mountain, thus very few people came to visit us. For this reason, life here was very quiet and peaceful. However, people had to work very hard on these farms.

Before my birth, my parents had lived in another village, but because of the war, my family had to move from place to place many times. The last place they came to live was the hamlet where I was born. The other two houses in the hamlet were my uncle's house and that of a neighbor. At the neighbor's, an old woman lived with her grandson and granddaughter. Her grandchildren were about my age. A very long time ago, she and her husband had lived here, but during that period when this village was not very secure there had been some fighting and her husband had been killed. After burying her husband she, together with her son, moved to Da Nang, one of the busiest cities in central Vietnam, in order to take up life again. When her son grew up, he joined the army and served for a few years, then he was killed in a battle. He left a wife, a son, and a daughter. Later on, when the village became more secure, the old woman decided to return to her old village to live, in order to take

Life in a new country is tough, but not so tough you can't smile.
Photo by Steve Long.

care of her husband's grave. Moreover, she wished to be buried beside her husband. Her daughter-in-law had to work as a small merchant to get some money to take care of the family so she stayed in Da Nang; however, her children followed their grandmother to the village to help her.

In my uncle's house, there were five people: my uncle, his wife, and their three sons. My uncle had been in the army for fifteen years. During his time of service, he had to move very often following orders; his family also moved many times following him. When he retired because of age, my mother asked him to move to this village to live, and he agreed.

In my house, there were thirteen people: my grandmother, my mother, and eleven children. My grandmother was very old so she did not work at all. My mother liked to work in farming more than as a merchant, thus she stayed on to work in the village after my father was killed in 1975 while in the army. Like most Vietnamese women, my mother worked very hard from six o'clock in the morning to five in the afternoon. She worked until midnight doing household chores. However, my family was not very wealthy. My older brothers and sisters had to go to the city to study because there was no high school in the small village. My mother had to provide them with money.

When I was young, in addition to going to school, I usually helped my mother working in the fields, going to the mountain to get dry wood, or going to the rivers to fish. On moonlit nights, I usually got together with some friends in the hamlet to play games such as hiding, jumping rope, or turning somersaults. Even though I did not have many friends in the hamlet, I had a lot of fun when we were together. In February 1975, the Vietnamese Communists tried to take over the country. My family, therefore, moved south, but when we were in Da Nang, some cities between Da Nang and Sai Gon had battles so we could not move any further by bus. Da Nang fell to the Communists about a month after we moved there. A month later the Communists took over the whole country. We could not run away from them, so my family returned to the hamlet. Under the new government, life was very difficult for everybody. People had to work very hard and had no free time and no rights. For myself, I had to spend more time working than having a good time with my young friends outside. My village, as well as the other villages in the country, daily became poorer. In 1975, I was in sixth grade, and I continued going to school until I was in the eleventh grade, which was 1980. During that period, I realized that I could not go to college after finishing high school. When I was eighteen years old I had to go in the army. I did not have any rights such as traveling or talking with friends. I was frightened by the Communist officials whenever I saw them because they could do whatever they wanted to me. There were many young men who were killed by them without a reason (as we later saw in the film *The Killing Fields*). I therefore decided to escape from the country.

In the summer of 1980, I joined some of my good friends to organize an escape. We bought a boat, five twenty-liter cans of fuel, some dried foods, and some antiseasickness medicines, and we planned to escape from the bottom of a mountain cliff beside the sea at three o'clock in the morning of June 15, 1980. On June 14, some of us who were not fishermen began to go to the cliff at nine o'clock in the evening. Some others who were fishermen did not have to go to the cliff because it was their duty to take the boat out from the river to the base of the cliff to get us. This was because when fishermen went out from the river to the sea to fish, they had to check out at a police station which was located at the mouth of the river. If anyone was not a fisherman he would not be allowed to go to sea. After fishing, the fishermen had to moor their boats in the river. That was why we had to go to the cliff. On the way to the cliff, we had to pass another police station to get to the foot of the mountain. We then climbed up the mountain. After getting to the top, we took a break for a while and then began to descend down to the base to wait for the boat. In the darkness of night, we had a very hard time getting there. When we arrived, our clothes were torn and our faces scratched, but we were very happy because we had almost made our escape. Unfortunately, although it was three o'clock, the boat did not appear. We waited for another hour and still did not see the boat. We slowly lost hope. At five o'clock, we had completely given up hope. We climbed back up the mountain in a hurry to go home before sunrise, hoping that no one would know we had tried to escape. However, we got caught on the way home by the police and we were sent to jail after we were punished with a beating. Later, I knew that the boat was not allowed to go out to sea that morning because the police thought that my friends were going to escape.

Living in jail, we had to work hard and did not get enough food, so we were always hungry. We had to have meetings every night, and in jail they did not provide beds, so we had to sleep on sand. I was then twenty. About a month later, my mother paid some money to some officials in hopes that they would let me go back home to visit my family. I received a permit to go home for a few days. When I was home, another friend of mine came over to ask me to try to escape again. She told me that her friends had already organized everything and it would be very safe. I agreed, but I had to wait three more days to escape; however, my permit from jail would expire on the next day. So I went to my relative's house in another village to hide. When the day came, I wanted to see my family before I left so I decided to go back to my house that night. I took the seven o'clock bus to go home at night so no one would know me. Unfortunately, right after I got off the bus, an officer saw me by accident, and he took me to his office. This time I was not afraid of him but worried about missing the appointment to escape. I tried to implore him to release me. I promised him that I would go back to jail the next day. For the first three hours, he said "no" and also warned me that he would punish me. However, I kept trying. Finally, he released me at midnight. I was so glad and went home in big hurry. When I got home, my mother was not yet asleep but all my brothers and sisters were sleeping. I talked with my mother for a while, then I left. While I was leaving my house, I looked back for one last time. My mother, an old lady whom I have respected since I was a little boy, was standing near the front door and looking at me to see me off. A feeling of melancholy came over me, together with commiseration with her feelings at that moment. But I had to go. I kept on and left my mother behind. This picture is engraved deeply in my mind.

Indeed, my friend was right; this time it was very safe even though we had to pass many dangerous places. The boat left Vietnam at one in the morning on August 1, 1980, and headed in a northeastern direction. The weather was not too cold, but the wind blew hard. Waves splattered us with sea water as they lapped against the boat. I was very cold. I had nothing to cover myself with. My body was always wet. The boat was small but there were many people in it. We had one seat for each person and we had to sit instead of lying down in the boat during the time we were on the ocean.

Five hours later, the sun began to rise. It became quiet; the wind did not blow hard and it was very cool. I did not see any islands or mountains around. One half of the sun rose above the ocean. In the sky, seagulls were flying and hunting fish. The red of the sunlight reflected from the surface of the sea made the surroundings very beautiful. The sun rose higher, but many people in the boat still slept because they were very tired and dizzy. Dangers and difficulties always threatened us during the time on the ocean. But right then I felt happy, because many Vietnamese who escaped toward the southeast had dangers and difficulties. They had to deal with pirates, who always stole, raped, and killed people. At about three o'clock in the afternoon of that day, we saw a mountain and believed that it was an island. We tried to approach it to get food and fuel if possible because we had not brought a lot. We had enough food and fuel for only one day. Indeed, it was a Chinese island, and we landed on this island at about six o'clock in the afternoon. The people were poor. We had to give them watches and gold rings to get fuel and food. We stayed there two days. We each had to find our own food during those days. There were two ways to get food; anyone who had items to exchange could get food easily. Otherwise, it was necessary to beg food from the people on the island. I did not have any gold or watches and was also too shy to beg food so I did not eat anything for those two days. After leaving the first place on Hainan Island, we dropped into other places along the island and had the same situation. After twelve days at sea and at Hainan Island, we arrived in Hong Kong.

In Hong Kong, I worked in a radio factory to get money to live during the time that I was waiting to go to a third country, the United States. While in Hong Kong, I didn't know how to speak Chinese, but I had a job and worked well so I got good pay. About six months later, I flew to the United States. The agency which sponsored my coming to the United States was located in Boston. I went to high school there for one year, to finish the twelfth grade.

In the first few years of living in this country I had a lot of problems with my English. I could not understand clearly what people said to me. I was like a mute and deaf person with them. When I was in Vietnam I had learned English for a few years, but I had not spoken and written it outside of class. I learned only some very simple sentences during that period. In America, I tried very hard to study English in high school and in the summers. Besides the problem with English, I felt homesick. My family was still in Vietnam. I could not see them anymore and I could not figure out what and how they were doing. It was not easy to send letters to my family and many letters that I had sent were never delivered to them. I also could not receive many letters from them. Later on, my life slowly changed. I knew more English. I had more friends. I felt much better. After finishing high school, I attended the University of Massachusetts in Amherst.

Living in this country I feel very happy because I am free. I tried to seek freedom even if it meant dying. Also, I have had a chance to go to college to improve my knowledge. Finally, I wish that Vietnam were free so the Vietnamese people who are living there wouldn't be treated as machines who work for the government.

HUYNH HUU HIEU

The Price of Freedom

THE capital became very crowded and noisy, and schools closed. Teachers had to enlist in the army. A lot of noise came from guns, bombs, and rockets, and the sound of the cannons rang through Saigon. Once again the word "war" appeared in my mind. The fighting began the first of April and lasted until the last day of the month. Thirty years of civil war between North and South Vietnam were over. As a result, the Republican government of South Vietnam had ended. It was replaced by a Communist government.

During that day, I and many other people in the city were lining the streets and cheering to greet the new government. The Communist soldiers were polite even though they had been fighting the South for thirty years. We thought that from now on we would have peace in Vietnam and that our families would be reunited. But, unfortunately, we were wrong. A few days later the Communists ordered that all the people who were officials of the old government were to be put in reeducation camps. My father was one of those victims. From that time, my family lived day to day, waiting for news of my father.

The Communists applied a cruel policy to the south. For example, every family had to have at least one person volunteer to work without pay for the government, otherwise that family would not have the opportunities that other families who worked "voluntarily" would have. For instance, they could not buy rice from the government. They had to buy it on the black market at an expensive price. Moreover, the new government forced the people in the city to move to the "New Economic Zones" which were located in underdeveloped regions.

This was a time of great significance in my life. I changed from the young boy I had been in high school into a person with an understanding of society and socialism. For example, after school I worked in the black market selling goods such as medical drugs and wrist watches, which was against the law. In order to help my family, I had to work hard. Every day I came home late and I did not spend a lot of time doing homework. My grades started going down. I was bored in school. There were many reasons for this. The school had begun to put more emphasis on studies in political areas. They also forced students to work for free for the government every weekend. If the students did not do the labor, they would be called bad students.

The courses in which I was previously interested now seemed unimportant to me. For example, in the English class the teacher had told us about America. I had written a paper twice, but still made a mistake on the word "liberty"; how could I write the word liberty correctly when my father was still in jail? Also, in the class on politics the teacher taught us of ways to develop the country, of socialism, and of ways to better the lives of our people. However, I could never understand why they did not teach us the way to liberty and the way to peace.

At the end of the semester, I received bad marks. I failed several courses such as politics and English. I was almost kicked out of school during that time and my mother had to promise the principal that I would do well in school. She did not force me to do anything, she just tried to give me a lot of encouragement. I wanted her to be happy, so I pretended to follow the school policy. I went to the classes, paid attention to the material, and did my homework every night. Later on, I received good grades, and completed my high school degree in 1979.

In 1979 the war between Vietnam and Cambodia got out of control. The Communist government of Vietnam forced all people who were eighteen years old to go into the armed services. The situation in the capital was very stressful. All the males seemed to have disappeared from the city. Some of them had been victims of the war or were still fighting it. The rest had fled the country. That did not mean they were shirking their duties of citizenship; it meant only that they did not like the idea of killing people and invading other countries. I was one of them.

On May 14, I went with my uncle's family to the province of Rach Gia to plan our escape from the country. This small village near the ocean was where we met the people who were leading those who wanted to escape. The leader arranged to let us stay there for a few days to wait for other groups of people and wait for the escape boat to return from a fishing expedition.

Finally, the day arrived. That night our family and fifty other people left the village following the leader to the boat. On the way there, we had to be quiet and hold hands so no one would get lost in the darkness.

After ten minutes we reached the shore. We saw the big fishing boat standing fifty feet from the shore. We felt happy and were ready for the journey. But when we approached the boat we were surrounded by a group of Communist soldiers. They commanded all of us not to move. If anyone tried to escape, he would be shot. They used a rope to tie all of us up and started to beat and search us for gold and jewelry. After they took all the valuables, they released us and made us go home.

Coming back home, I felt depressed and disappointed. My mother felt very sad, and she tried to find another group to send me with.

One day the chance came for me again. I packed my luggage and started for the second escape attempt. This time my mother was to accompany me to the boat. I said goodbye to my father, sister, and youngest brother. My father, who had finally been released from the reeducation camp, told me to try to study and make a living for myself in another country and not to forget our family.

This time, the place my mother took me was very familiar. It was my mother's province. We arrived there in the evening and spent the night in an uncle's house.

The next afternoon, my mother led me to the place where the boat was docked. The leader came to guide me on to the boat. I started to say good-bye to my mother. She cried a lot and hugged me in her arms. I felt very hurt inside because I had no idea what was in store for me in the future.

On the boat, I turned my head to look at my mother for one last time. Tears came pouring from her eyes. I wanted to run back to her arms, but the river separated us. In eighteen years with my family, I had received a lot of care and teaching from my parents and I had not had the chance to repay them. I wondered how I would ever be able to repay them for causing even more worries now that I was leaving them.

In the evening the boat was filled with people and it started heading out to sea. On the way our boat had to pass through a Communist patrol station. We had to follow the instructions of the leader, which were not to talk and to cover the children's mouths in case they cried, for it would signal to the soldiers that this was an escape boat. As our boat passed through their patrol station without trouble, all of us felt happy and thanked God.

After a few hours on the sea we all felt seasick from the stormy ocean waves, except for the captain. He seemed brave to us because he tried to save the boat amidst the ocean's anger. I was so exhausted from seasickness that I could not move my hands and did not recognize my surroundings. A few minutes later I was awakened by the yelling of some people around me. The boat was half filled with water and the engine had stopped. The boat would sink if nobody bailed the water out. I and a group of men had to use the last of our energies trying to save the boat and ourselves.

The morning broke with a beautiful ocean scene. The storm had stopped and I sat on board to relax from the horrible night. Now, as people started to go above deck to smell the fresh air, I saw my cousin among them. We counted forty-two people on the boat in all.

The captain announced to us that we were in territory that was under Communist control, so we needed to fix the boat to keep it going. After working all afternoon, we succeeded. The engine ran again to carry us out of Communist territory. We felt happy and free. We were still worried, however, since we did not know where we were heading. The engine went out again for sixteen hours, and we started to worry that we did not have enough food and water. The mechanic in our group tried to fix the engine but he gave us no hope at all. People on the boat tried to think up ideas. For instance, we suggested that the boat could be rowed. We tried to row it but it did not get far, and as a result of our work we were tired and exhausted. I thought we might remain like that on the sea until a storm came up and sank the boat. Then the sharks would have a delicious dinner.

The third day came with its hot temperature and dry scorching sun. Each person on the boat received only two cups of water per day. Some people began dissolving sugar into the sea water and

The first generation to grow up in America.
Photo by Sam Pettengill.

drinking it, but it still tasted terrible. Another group boiled the sea water to distill it. But all they would get would be a cup of water for two hours' worth of work.

The next day was filled with horror. Some women lost consciousness because they did not have enough water and food. Children cried for their mothers, husbands tried to make their unconscious wives drink the little amount of water allowed by the group leader. Very little water was left, and that was given to women and children. We were starved with hunger, thirst, and heat. People bathed with sea water to ease the pain of the scorching sun.

We floated on the sea for days and days. The ninth day arrived without our having seen a single boat on the sea. I thought that if we did not get rescued on that day, we would all die, because all the people on the boat were exhausted and weak, and water was leaking into the boat. We were losing strength, and were barely able to bail out the boat. If no one bailed it out, the boat would sink.

Fortunately, that same day, we spotted a big ship on the horizon, heading toward our boat. As it came nearer, we saw the banner with red and white stripes and stars on a blue background. Then we knew we were saved; it was an American ship.

After the Americans loaded our frail bodies onto the ship, where we received medical care and light nourishment, they took us to the small island of Pulau Bidong, in Malaysia, where we found shelter. I stayed there for six months, until I was given permission to come to the United States with my father and brother, who had later arrived on the island.

Since then, my whole family has made the dangerous journey to the United States, and all have arrived on these shores safely. I am happy and thankful that my whole family has been able to establish a new life in this country. I will never forget those nine desperate days on open seas. The price of freedom is great.

LE TAN SI

A Terrifying Escape

My native village is Phu An, where my parents were born. My father and mother married when both of them were eighteen years old. After five years of marriage, they settled in Saigon in 1955. My mother bore five children, three boys and two girls, and I am the fourth child. My parents were fruit merchants when they lived in Saigon. My family's religion is Confucianism. My brothers, sisters, and I went to school as my parents wished, since my father and mother had not had an opportunity to go to school when they were young because they had to help their families in business. In other words, both parents completed only the second year of elementary school. They wanted us to gain a good education. Therefore, all the boys were sent to a famous private school, La San Taberd, in Saigon. French was the foreign language that I studied in my school. Unfortunately for my sisters, they failed the test in junior high, so they left school and helped my parents in business. When I was young, my mother told me that if I completed the tenth grade, she would give me some money to travel with my friends; therefore, I tried to study hard in order to earn the grade my mother expected of me.

I lived with my family during the peaceful time. But on April 30, 1975, the Vietnamese Communists occupied Saigon. I was in the ninth grade. Half of the students in my school left the country on April 30 or before; after that, the others gradually left, except my brothers and me. The war ended and we thought that peace had come to our country. But it was not so. My family began going separate ways.

After 1975, my father returned to his village to take care of his farm. My older brother planned to flee the country with his friends, but my mother did not want him to leave our family, so he stayed with us. For four years we lived under the Vietnamese Communist government. We noticed that we had no freedom, but my family kept the word "freedom" in mind during the period of Communist rule. My parents tried to find a way to flee the country; in my family, I was the first person to try my luck. On June 4, 1979, I left my country and family for freedom, and then passed through a terrible ordeal.

Around 9:00 P.M. on June 4, 1979, our boat departed in good weather with fifty-eight people on board. Our boat operated safely for the next two days. However, although I had paid for my trip I starved on those days. The trip was full of hardship. Around 2:00 A.M. on June 6, 1979, the overworked engine broke down. Our boat drifted downwind, and so did my life. During this period, I left my life to chance. Early the morning of June 7, the weather changed suddenly. It was raining and the wind was blowing and, because our boat's engine was broken, the boat bobbed up and down with the waves. We were frightened because we had no control over our boat with a dead engine; we prayed to God for help in the heavy rain. Meanwhile, we anchored to make the boat safer. I thought and thought about my life, parents, and friends, and I also wondered if my death was near. Our supply of food and water was gradually decreasing as our boat drifted on the sea, so we starved. We prayed for a savior who could help and rescue us from this hardship.

Around 11:00 A.M. that day, a strange boat came toward our boat. It was a Thai boat in which there were six Thai fishermen. The Thai fishermen tried to help us repair our engine, but they were not able to; however, they took our engine apart. Then they gave us lunch and some cans of water, and they told us that they would help us. By noon, the Thai fishermen towed our boat to Malaysia after they and Vinh, the boat's owner, talked over our situation.

Our boat passed into Thailand's territorial waters. Ten minutes later, the Thai "fishermen" displayed guns, knives, and hooks in order to frighten us. We understood then that the Thai fishermen were pirates. They quickly took our valuables, such as rings, earrings, chains, watches, and bracelets, because they saw another boat coming toward us. Perhaps the pirates were afraid that it might have been a Thai patrol boat, so they left right after they robbed us. However, this other boat was also a fishing boat. They passed by our boat without pity; in fact, they laughed at us, because they perceived that we had been robbed recently. I had not been robbed by the pirates, because I had hidden my gold ring in my mouth, but I was a little scared by the pirates. Almost all of us were flabbergasted at the recent occurrence. We understood that we were faced with Thai pirates and would probably die next time.

"Thai pirates" are words I will never forget for the rest of my life. I don't like to remember why. In fact, they were simple fishermen but they availed themselves of the opportunity of becoming pirates. More than one thousand Vietnamese were killed or committed suicide when confronted by such robbers. From the Vietnamese newspaper I learned that pirates captured over one hundred Vietnamese girls and women and took them to a deserted island to rape them. Some of those females killed themselves. Others contracted venereal disease. The pirates raped the Vietnamese girls and women on our boats, and killed the people who struggled with them.

While I was deep in thought in the cabin, there was a strange boat that came rapidly toward us. I was frightened by that boat, because it moved directly toward us. I was numb with fear. I could not move. I only sat and stared at that boat. The boat moved closer toward me. . . . That boat was twenty yards away from me, and it was ten yards, . . . then five yards, and I closed my eyes. Ugh! I wondered how lucky I would be. That boat changed direction and it passed the stern, splashing water so that half our boat was flooded. The pirates, the same we had encountered that morning, jumped aboard. I was the first person who dove into the ocean when I heard someone call "jump," and then others followed. I was in the water a few minutes with fear, because I realized that if I stayed long in the ocean I might be a shark's prey, so my people and I swam back to our boat. Then the pirates checked everyone elaborately and robbed some more of our valuables. Next, the pirates ordered us to get in the front of our boat, where almost all the people fainted from gasoline vapors. The owner of our boat told us that someone had emptied out the gas tank because he wanted to be supported with that tank in the sea.

Those real situations made me think about death, which seemed to lessen my own energy. Besides, I thought that if I were to have an easy death I would have to pass out. Pass out . . . the phrase haunted my mind continually until I heard someone laughing. The laughter became fainter and fainter in my ears, and I lost consciousness.

The day after, I woke up and I was very happy that I had not died that night. The pirates left us an hour after they had robbed us. Then I went back to the cabin and found my ring, which I had thrown into the engine room. So I was not robbed the second time either. After that, I had my property in the corner of our boat. I felt starved again, so I thought in my starved mind that the pirates came to us, because we had some food and water.

Around 10:30 A.M. on June 9, other pirates came to rob us, and they gave us some food and water. They left us after they took a gold ring from us, but they refused to help us by towing our boat to land or to Malaysia. We despaired and could not do anything with our boat, so everyone prayed again to God to help us. A few hours later it rained, so we had some rainwater by using a parachute to catch it. The rain stopped around 3:00 P.M., but we had no control over our boat. We would sail by the parachute, and our boat would drift to our country or Cambodia in one or two weeks, but we would probably die of starvation before then while our boat floated on the sea. No one had a choice. Everyone's life was left to chance. Fortunately, a Thai boat came toward us after we sailed about ten minutes. They were saviors. They let us have a night on their boat, gave us some soup and water, and tried to repair our engine. Before I slept, I checked my ring for security, and I saw some Thai fishermen check our property. I was silent. On June 10, the Thai fishermen drew our boat to Malaysia. When we spotted the Malaysian islands, they left us after they gave us some food and water. Then we thanked God and our saviors from the bottom of our hearts before we joyfully sailed our boat to Malaysia.

We arrived at the shore about 5:00 P.M. on June 11, and our engine was broken again. We then stopped at the Malaysian seashore and spent a night there. During our time on the island, we exchanged gasoline for some food, packs of cigarettes, and water. Next day, June 12, a Malaysian patrol boat came toward us and towed us toward them. The captain promised us that they would take us to the Malaysian refugee camp on the next day; we were pleased with that news. There were also two other Vietnamese boats that came in that night. We were gratified when we saw a great many Vietnamese people, so all of us spent the night on our boats.

About 10:00 A.M. on June 13, the patrol boat's captain refused to guide our boats to their refugee camp, because their government had stopped accepting refugees. There were about thirty thousand

Vietnamese refugees in the refugee camp, so the camp was full. Then the captain ordered his patrol boat to tow our boats to Singapore. That news disappointed us and struck us with consternation. Two of our boats were towed by the Malaysian patrol boat. The Malaysian navy ordered the Vietnamese people on the third boat out of that boat, and those people moved into our two boats because the Malaysians wanted to take one of our three boats. The captain of the patrol boat told us through a megaphone that it would take forty-eight hours to get to Singapore. However, they towed us for only about thirty hours; then they left us after they told us to navigate our boats to some islands. We again resigned ourselves to our fate. I thought about death again because our engine was broken. I asked myself where I would have been even then, if the other boat had not rescued the people on our boat. Fortunately, the boat owner let us get on his boat to continue the last part of our journey. Then we directed the boat toward those unknown islands. In my case, I was very unhappy when I stared at my boat drifting on the sea. I thought that it would sink with my pair of shoes. I stared and stared at it until it was out of sight, and then I came near to crying.

Finally, our boat came to the unknown islands about 9:00 P.M. on June 14. I saw that there were many Vietnamese people on those islands, and then I learned that I had arrived in Indonesia. I really had survived, because I was a legal refugee in the Indonesian refugee camp when I landed on those islands.

I had a miraculous escape, but my mind was still haunted by death. I did not lose my golden ring, which helped me buy some food in the refugee camp. In January 1980, approval was given for me to migrate to the United States. I lived in the KuKu and Galang refugee camps for fourteen months under the support of the United Nations. On August 20, 1980, I set foot in Seattle. I then really had freedom and a new life in this country. After a month of living in Arlington, Texas, I received a letter from the Galang refugee camp and I learned that my older brother had arrived there. I was very happy. Six months later, my brother came to Boston with his wife. When my brother's family arrived in Boston, my brother asked me to live with them. There I would be able to continue my education. So I moved to Boston on March 15, 1981. I graduated from Brighton High School and then I attended the University of Massachusetts, Amherst.

DANG HONG LOAN

A Tragic Voyage

I met with a young girl Ly whom I interviewed. In disbelief I learned of her tragic journey from Vietnam to Thailand which has left her with a painful scar.

Before the fall of Saigon in 1975 Ly was the happiest girl. She was the only daughter of a respected physician. Being a well-known physician, her father had been able to provide her with a good life, a life that many girls her age wished for. In school she always wore the nicest clothes. At home she had the cutest dolls of all her friends. But when the North Vietnamese took the south, her father, like many other high-ranking officials, including those who had been associated with the American government, were sent to the north (to camps). She and her mother had to move in with one of her aunts. Access to education was denied her because of her father's past. Life for her became a shattered dream. Now she could only watch in tears as her friends walked to school. She had to stay home helping her mother bake cakes to sell at a nearby market so that they could have money to buy clothes and medicine to send to her sick father in the "reeducation" camp. Her clothes which used to be the prettiest were now faded and mended in several places.

Ly's father was allowed to return home after three long years in the camp. Ly cried a lot at the sight of her father's condition. Once a strong, healthy, and confident man, he was now just a very sick old man who had suffered malnutrition and bad treatment. For him, three years in the reeducation camp had been like thirty. Most of his hair

Dang Hong Loan, vice president of the University of Massachusetts Vietnamese Students Association. Photo by Steve Long.

had turned gray, which made him look very old. After his recovery, he and his wife, who worried for their daughter's future, planned an escape for her to a foreign country where they hoped she would have a better chance for a future. After several attempts and failures, one rainy night her single uncle took her on a small boat with about sixty other people and they headed for freedom. Ly was used to many good-byes by now, but this time she had the feeling that this was going to be the last she would ever see her parents. Her parents must have felt the same way because her mother held Ly back for a long time. Finally, her father had to pull her away and gave her the last embrace before she went with her uncle. She was then twelve years old.

They had been at sea two days and they had been lucky because there were no high waves or strong winds, even though it was September. They had enough food and water for a week. Their stomachs would not go hungry and their throats would not go dry from the heat of the sun. They could only eat and drink a small amount. Ly had never cried as much as she did on the first day. She felt homesick, she felt lost in the big sea, she felt tiny and scared. The next day, there were some problems with the engine, but her uncle and two other men were able to fix it. Then it broke again the next day. This time they were helpless as they waited for someone to pass by. As night grew darker, some of the women and Ly started to cry for fear. The men just sat there looking into the dark, hoping to see some lights or something moving so they could have something to hope for.

The next morning, they saw a larger boat moving with high speed toward them. Everybody cried out for joy. Some of them even stood up on the boat and waved and that caused the boat to rock back and forth vigorously. Ly was also happy, but as she looked at her uncle she sensed something was terribly wrong. The smile on his face quickly disappeared and was replaced by a look of fear. She followed his eyes to the other boat that came near to her little boat and sent strong waves to one side of it. Her uncle recognized the strange boat as belonging to pirates. He warned everyone on the boat about pirates. She saw the men on the other boat were armed with knives, and they yelled to the people on her boat in a strange language. A loud thud brought everybody back to reality as the large boat pulled over and hit her boat on one side. Water started to pour in through the big hole caused by the impact. With unfriendly gestures, the men on the other boat forced everybody into the corner of the boat. Two men from the strange boat jumped on her boat and started to search for valuable items. At the same time those men began to personally search the victims. A man fought back and was killed immediately. His body was thrown to the sea as others looked on in terror. Those wicked men laughed at each other as they attacked the women. After the search, they forced everybody but six girls and Ly onto their boat. That was the last she saw of her uncle. She was kept separate in the cabin, away from the other six girls. An older man, probably the captain, brought her food every day. At night she slept in terror as she heard the screams and begging for mercies from the other girls and the lustful laughs of the wicked men. She did not know what was going on, but in her young mind she knew that it must have been something very terrible. The third night after watching her finish her meal, the old man attacked and raped her. She fought with all her might, but what could a twelve-year-old girl do to stop a grown man from attacking her? After raping her several times, he left her lying unconscious. The next day she had a high fever. The old man tried to feed her some food but she could not eat anything and was scared by his touches. Even the shadow of him sent her quivering into the corner of the bed. The fifth day, after attacking another refugee boat and ransacking it for valuable belongings, the pirates let the men, the children, and the elderly back into their old boat. The old man forced one of the victims to take Ly back with him into the refugee boat. Two days later, they landed in Thailand and arrived at Songkla refugee camp the same day. Ly was admitted to the hospital and stayed there for more than two weeks. In her case, she was lucky; nobody ever heard of what had happened to the other six girls that were captured at the same time with Ly.

Eight months after her discharge from the hospital, through a program to help single children resettle, Ly was adopted by an American couple and came to the United States in 1982. Now Ly is a straight A student but she rarely smiles. Behind her sad eyes is a memory of a tragic journey that changed her life. Occasionally, one finds her staring blankly at nothing in particular as tears come rolling down from her eyes. Is she thinking about her parents or about her sad experiences? Nobody seems to know.

LAM PHU

A Vietnamese-Born Chinese

My name is Lam Phu and I am a student at the University of Massachusetts in Amherst. My major is electrical engineering. I would like to tell you some of my family background. My father and mother came from an island southeast of China called Hainan. I still do not know when they came to Vietnam, but I know that they met in Saigon and were married there. After they got married, they moved to Banmethuot, which is a town in the central part of Vietnam, and they had a business there. My family is large. I have six older brothers, three older sisters and a younger brother. Including my parents, there are thirteen of us.

When we were young, my parents sent us to the Chinese school in town to study. The books we used in school were from Taiwan. I spoke Mandarin in school to my teachers. At home I spoke the Hainanese dialect to my parents. I spoke Vietnamese to my brothers and sisters and to my friends. I did not learn to read and write Vietnamese when I was in elementary school.

After the Communists took over South Vietnam in 1975, my school was closed for a while and then reopened. At that time, the school did not teach Chinese anymore and I had to learn the Vietnamese language. Since I had never learned Vietnamese, it was difficult for me to study it in the beginning. However, I was able to read and write Vietnamese well after two years of studying hard.

On March 10, 1975, I woke up early in the morning as usual and prepared for school. My mother stopped me at the door and told me that there was no school that day. I was unhappy about it. When I went back to my room, my father told me not to go anywhere because fighting was going on outside. Communist soldiers were in town. They had been fighting with the South Vietnamese army since one o'clock in the morning. Because I had slept very well the night before, I had not been aware of what was going on that morning. Once in a while, I heard some gunfire in my community. I liked that atmosphere, however, because usually nobody went anywhere, and normally the streets were empty. The sounds reminded me of the Chinese New Year. The next morning, I heard many guns and shells firing around the town. It went on like that for three days, and it seemed to me that they were fighting hard outside. Suddenly, a bomb was dropped next to my house. Then it exploded. Everything shook like an earthquake. I smelled gunpowder. Smoke and broken pieces of glass flew over my head. I was afraid of what was going on and my mother told us to lie down on the floor. Fortunately, nobody in my family was wounded in that explosion.

My father decided to move to a safer place, and so my family moved to my school. On my way to school, I saw many houses burning in town. Dead bodies lay in the streets. I had seen many movies with pictures like that before, but since they had been just movies, I had not had much feeling about it. But this time it was different. I was experiencing a real war in my life. Not only could I see it, but I also could smell and touch it. I was afraid then. Afraid that I would die or that someone in my family would die. We arrived at my school and many people were already there. The next morning, a Communist soldier came to my classroom. He told us to stay where we were and not to go anywhere because it was dangerous outside.

The fighting went on for about one week. Then the Communist soldiers took total control of my town. I felt better when there was no more fighting. I saw many Communist soldiers who were very polite when they talked to the older people in my school. They helped wounded children to the hospital and cleaned up the streets after the war. At that time, I thought that they must be good people.

Even though the fighting had ceased in my town, people from Saigon kept sending their airplanes to drop bombs over our heads. Once again, my town was on fire. Communist soldiers asked us to evacuate the town and go to a plantation. After fifty-two days of continuous fighting, on April 30, Communist soldiers captured Saigon and they celebrated their victory.

My father was a businessman and did not like politics. No one in my family had ever been involved with the South Vietnamese government. At that time, I was too young to understand the system which I lived in before 1975. Also, I was too young to understand the feeling of some Vietnamese who had fought and even died for the independence of South Vietnam in the struggle against the Communists from the north.

When the Communists took control of South Vietnam in 1975, I had no idea who they might be or what they might do. They began their propaganda. Everything they said seemed reasonable to me. They were very positive when they told us about communism. From their propaganda, I knew that the South Vietnamese government had collapsed. Moreover, in the past the society of South Vietnam had favored a small group of people who were rich and who had power. Poor people, on the other hand, who had to work hard could not earn enough for a living. People were forced to join the army in South Vietnam. They said that under the Communist government, Vietnam was united. There would be no more war, no more injustice, and no criminals in the society. They told us that it was time for change in our society for a better future. People had to work hard for themselves and be independent from foreign countries. I was enthusiastic about the Communist ideals of life. I worked hard in school as well as in my community. I was happy because I could help people build a better future based on socialism. My life was full of promise.

As has been said before, "Nothing good lasts forever." It was true. At the end of 1978, the Chinese invaded Vietnam's northern part. Since I was active in school, it was possible that they would ask me to join the army and then send me to the frontier to fight against the Chinese. It was a duty that I would not perform, that I could not perform. Although I was born in Vietnam and had grown up in that country, and my parents had become Vietnamese citizens while living in Vietnam, my father always reminded me that I was Chinese rather than Vietnamese. Sometimes he told me about his family. He also told me about the village where he had lived in China and asked me to memorize the address. In the town, the Communists were very tough on the Chinese merchants. They took away their property and sometimes sent them to jail. What they did seemed reasonable to me because in order to achieve socialism it was necessary to abolish capitalism. Things like that had happened in China during the Cultural Revolution. I did not react

Fishing in the old country, a livelihood as well as a pastime.
Photo by Joel M. Halpern.

much at that time. The Vietnamese Communists started their campaign against China at school and on the radio. They said many bad things about China. In addition, they showed photographs of Chinese soldiers who had invaded Vietnam and died at the front. It made me feel uncomfortable when I was in school as well as when I was on the streets.

The Vietnamese Communists viewed the Chinese who lived in Vietnam as a threat to their national security. They were afraid that the more than one million Chinese who lived in Vietnam would support the Communists in China by getting together to start internal chaos, then perhaps overthrow the Vietnamese government. Something like that would be very unlikely. However, the Vietnamese Communists thought it was possible that their government could be overthrown by the Chinese, which would make it easier for the Communists in China to push at the border in the northern part of Vietnam. Moreover, many Chinese in Vietnam were wealthy people, and the Vietnamese Communists thought that by allowing them to leave Vietnam, the Communist government could exact a certain amount of money. When the Chinese left Vietnam, their properties would no longer belong to them but to the Vietnamese government. Under those conditions, the Vietnamese Communists allowed the Chinese in Vietnam to go back to China or to another country.

In the spring of 1979, my family planned to leave Vietnam. There were two ways for me to go. The first one was to the north and from there into China. The second one was to the south and from there to Malaysia. While everybody in my family wanted to go to Malaysia, I asked my mother if she could help me go to China. I did not want to go to the capitalist world because I thought that there were injustices and many criminals there. Since I could not live well with the Communists in Vietnam, I might as well live with the Communists in China. Moreover, China is the land of my ancestors. My mother told me that I was young and had to follow my older brothers and sisters. I agreed to go with them.

It was not easy for my family to leave Vietnam. We knew that it would be hard for us to escape from that country. As a matter of fact, two of my brothers had tried several times to escape and had not succeeded. Therefore, we could leave only if the Communists would allow us to go officially. We also needed to have money to pay the government and to pay for our transportation. It was a large amount of money and my family could not afford to pay for the whole family to leave Vietnam at the same time. Since we lived in the highlands, we could not directly contact people who had organized to leave Vietnam, so we moved south to look for such an organization. There, people were very tricky; we needed to contact the right people, or else we could lose our money easily.

We did not escape; our boat was actually given permission to leave Vietnam after we paid a certain amount of money to the government. On April 30, 1979, after four years of living under Communist rule, my family left Vietnam heading south to Malaysia. I missed my school, my teachers, and all my friends.

Our boat was overcrowded with more than three hundred people. It was hard for people to go anywhere on the boat. During the three days at sea, we were attacked several times by pirates. They did not kill or rape anyone, but they took away our property. The boat was allowed to land in Malaysia, and the police took us to a refugee camp, where we stayed for eleven months. One of my brothers, who had left Vietnam in 1977 and had gone to the United States, was my family's sponsor in the United States.

My family came to the United States in March 1980. I had no idea what I would do in the future because this country was so new and strange to me. Because of my background, I did not trust capitalism. It was an unjust society where rich people were selfish and unfair to poor people. I did not like the idea of living in America. However, I had to follow the rest of my family to the United States. I met my older brother who was our sponsor. He told us that life in the United States was easy. We did not have to worry about food and clothing. He told me to go to school.

I started tenth grade at Brighton High School in Boston. I did very well in high school. I was an honors student. As a result, I was accepted at Brandeis University as an upwardbound student for summer school. It was the first time that I had to leave my family and live at the university with many American students. I was afraid then. In my first summer at Brandeis I had some problems with my roommate who was Spanish. First of all, I did not speak English well enough to make people understand me. While I was studying hard, my roommate was hanging around with his friends. They turned on music and sometimes they smoked marijuana. I could not stand the smoke and so much noise. I told him to quiet down a little, but he did not listen to me. He said that that was the way people lived in the United States. I did not believe what he said. However, there was nothing I could do to stop him from what he was doing. That summer only lasted for six weeks and I went back home to my family.

I went back to Brandeis the next summer. That time I had a single room. Like the first summer, I studied hard, but it did not work. Maybe I did not get along well with American students. Since I could not adapt to this society, I felt isolated. American students taught me how to dance. They took me to the swimming pool and to a party. Sometimes they told me about their families, but I had nothing to tell them about myself and about the country where I came from. I did not think people wanted to hear about Vietnam and what was going on over there. I had energy and motivation. I would have liked to participate in many activities in school, as I had done before in Vietnam after 1975. I would have liked to be friendly with American students. I would have liked to speak to them and to understand how they felt. But I could not do it, because we were different in so many ways, and I could not change myself to adapt to this society. The reason was that I was not one of them. I was not an American. I felt homesick. I missed my school in Vietnam. I missed my teachers and all my friends. I just wanted to go home. No matter how hard I tried in my studying, it did not work.

After I came to the United States, I started to change my political point of view. In high school, I took two political science courses. It was the first time I had had a chance to compare and contrast capitalism and communism. I did not have a chance like that when I was in Vietnam. I started to understand the capitalist system. It was not as bad as I thought. In addition, I saw some Chinese movies from Taiwan talking about family tragedies caused by the Communists on mainland China, and recently I saw *The Killing Fields*. It makes me think that communism is not as good as I thought it was. Communists are against human nature and they are inhuman. As a matter of fact, in Vietnam after ten years under Communist rule, people are still poor. People are still fighting in Cambodia. There is no peace in that country as had been promised by the Communists. China today, thirty-five years after the Communist Revolution, is still one of the poorest countries in the world. Communist China does not do well economically. People in that country are poor and they are behind many Western countries.

The theory of communism is more idealistic than realistic. In many Communist societies, it is propaganda that motivates people to work hard for their countries. Sometimes it does not work, since people are selfish. There are not many people who are willing to work hard for the commonwealth of their society when they get nothing in return for themselves and their family. Moreover, Communists do not want their citizens to develop freely through education, because they are afraid that if their citizens get smarter than they, it will be hard for officials to control their citizens. Consequently, the Communists execute scholars and promote the laboring class in the society. Without professional people working for them, and without citizens willing to work hard for the society, Communist countries cannot develop well economically, and as a result, many cannot catch up with some Western countries.

A progressive society is one where people are free to compete with each other. People are always trying to find a way to do things better. In order to improve their lives, people work to produce more goods of better quality. They get paid for their labor. Money generally has provided a better living for many people and their families. Since many people would like to earn more money, they are willing to work hard every day in the United States. Here, on this campus, I work hard as an engineering student to get a bachelor's degree in science in the near future. I may not achieve my goal, however, I have studied hard. The more I study, the more I see that I am not as good a student as I thought. This brings me back to the realization that I need to study more than I have studied before. I am optimistic about my future, since I believe that if I try hard enough, some day I will get what I want.

NGUYEN HUU CHUNG

Separation and Reunion

I was born on February 13, 1965, in Saigon. I am the sixth oldest of nine children in my family. My family lived in Bac-Hai, Ho-Nai, which is a small town about 100 kilometers from Saigon. My father was a truck driver. He was the only one working to support the family. As I recall, when we lived in Vietnam we could be best described as a middle-class family.

Since birth I have had a very curious mind. I always asked questions about things that I was uncertain of or did not understand. For instance, one time one of our neighbors had a wedding. I did not know the meaning of this ceremony, so I asked my mother, "Mom, why and how do people have such a ceremony?" She explained, "The reason we have this is because, when two people are in love, they want to have this celebration so that they can form a new family for a new generation." Being so curious, I started to investigate this answer. Later on, I found out that only part of her answer was true. I found out that most marriages were arranged by the parents of the groom. In other words, the parents of the groom had to visit the bride's parents and arrange the marriage. Then if the bride's parents agreed, the groom would be allowed to see the bride and get acquainted. Afterward, the groom's parents would arrange for the wedding, which usually took place after about a year.

Besides having a curious mind, I was also a very alert young man. I always observed anything that happened in the village. For example, I noticed that the fathers of the family were all working, the

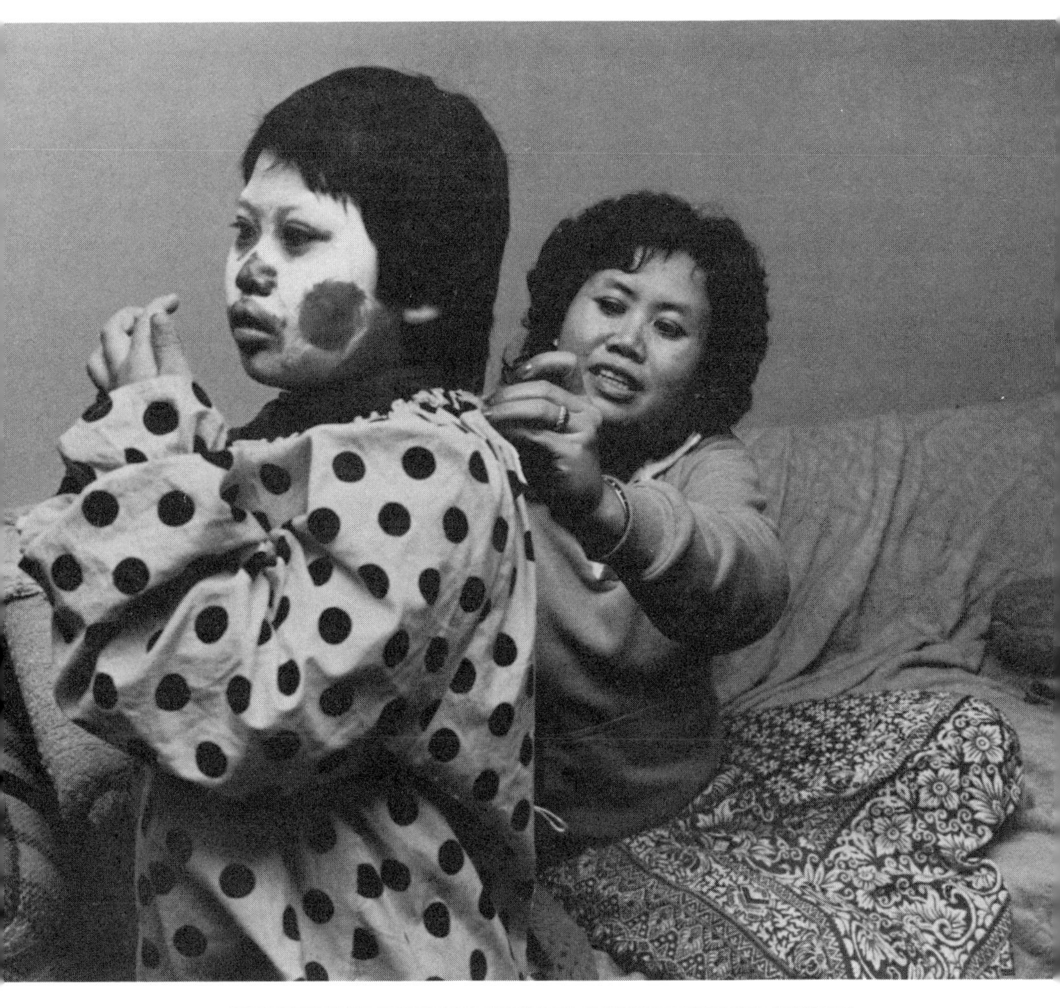

“My son wants to dress in the American way for Halloween.” Photo by Sam Pettengill.

mothers took care of the children, and the sons went to school. The daughters also went to school but they all quit when they got out of high school. The reason for this was that in my country we believed that women's jobs were to raise the children. Therefore, they did not need to get a higher education. This kept women from competing with men for jobs. I also noticed that most of the older parents who could not work any more lived with the oldest son in the family. Thus, the oldest son was considered to be the most important member in the family. He was responsible for his parents when they became elderly. Also, if the parents died, he would take over the parents' responsibility in rearing all the younger family members.

Concerning my schooling, I must say that from the first grade through the third grade I did very well. I received A's in all of my courses, and I was never hit with a stick by any of my teachers. However, as soon as I got into the fourth grade, everything changed. I began to skip school and disobey all the teachers. When my father found out about this, he sent me away to a boarding school, where I had to stay for a whole month at a time. The first month I was there, I was so lonely and homesick that the Catholic sisters, who were watching over me, had to bring me home every week. But then day by day I got used to the school. The sisters were extremely nice and I considered them like my own parents. I stayed in this school for almost two years and then my father sent me back to the school near home. The reason was that he knew Saigon's fall was near and he wanted the whole family to stay together.

A month before the fall of Saigon, my father asked my oldest brother, Hien, an air force officer based at Tra Noc, to stay home and go with us to Vung Tau. My brother replied: "Father, if I were a soldier, I'd stay, but I am an officer and my responsibility is very great to my soldiers, so please forgive me." After that he drove the whole family to Vung Tau, and my family never saw him again.

Two days before the Communists attacked Saigon, my father and my third brother drove the truck to Saigon to do business. Then the Vietcong attacked Long Binh, a town centered between Saigon and Vung Tau. We—my mother, three sisters, three brothers, and I—lost contact with my father and did not know what to do, so we stayed behind. Meanwhile, my father and brother thought that when the Americans left Vung Tau they would take us along, so he and my brother boarded a boat at Saigon and left for America.

Without my father, we really had to struggle to survive.

My mother had to raise pigs. My two older sisters had to go to the black market selling beans and rice, and I had to push a two-wheeled cart and carry anything that the businessmen wanted. Boy! I tell you I really grew up fast! I never had a chance to go to school anymore, and many of the villagers looked down on me. Times were very hard and my mother had to save every penny we had so that we could leave Vietnam.

After a year of living under communism, we received a letter from my father saying that he and my brother were doing fine and were praying that our family would be reunited. A few months later we received a package from him. In this package there were fabrics, medicines, clothes, and canned foods. Instead of using these medicines, clothes, and fabrics, we sold all of them to get money. Then we wrote to my father and asked him to send some more packages. He sent one package every four months and we did not need to go to work anymore and were much better off. Some villagers began to look up to us, now that we were doing better, including some of the soldiers from the north. However, my mother didn't trust them. She knew that all of them were greedy, and so she kept thinking that we had to leave the country and be reunited with my father and brother.

In order to leave the country, we had to give money to the boat owners so that they could make escape plans and prepare their boat. They asked for a lot of money, and after trying to save money for a year, we had only enough to pay for one person. By that time I was twelve years old. My mother looked around the room, then said to me: "My son, I have to let you go because if you stay, then soon you will have to go either to fight or to Kinh Te Moi (a reeducation program)." Then I replied: "But Mom, I can't, what about all of my friends?" She answered: "Soon, you will have no friends whether you stay or not." Afterward, she sent me down to Vung Tau, where I made my escape along with two of my cousins. These cousins of mine were also from Vung Tau. They wanted to leave the country simply because of the financial problems in their family: the Vietcong were about to take over all of their belongings.

We escaped in September 1978 on a small boat along with twenty-six other people. We were on the sea for three days. Then we saw another boat. At first we thought it was a rescue boat, but it turned out to be a Thai fishing boat. When they saw us, they began to approach us. Once we were in contact with their boat all of the men, who were armed with weapons, jumped over to our boat and began to strip us to search for gold. After that they began to rape all the women on board. I will never forget seeing all the men crying when they watched their wives being raped and were unable to do anything. One man could not take it any more, and he jumped up and tried to fight the Thai, but he was shot and killed by the Thai captain. After this they began to beat all the men and throw us overboard. My two cousins and I were hit on the head and were unconscious.

The next morning when I woke up, I saw only eighteen people left on board. Upon seeing this, I asked the captain where all of the people were. He replied that seven people died of drowning, one got shot, and three girls were taken as hostages on the Thai boat. He did not know what happened to those three girls! I then asked, "Where is the Thai boat?" He said, "They left last night and I hope they will never come back."

After the fifth day at sea we were rescued by the ship called *The Panama* which took us to the Pulau Bidong refugee camp. While living in this camp, my cousins and I experienced one of the most difficult times of our lives. We had an uphill battle chopping down trees to build a house and to make firewood for cooking. We had to be very independent because we had no friends and no relatives. After staying there for five months, my sister and brother arrived. When I first saw them I was so excited that tears came to my eyes. Then afterward I asked my sister about her trip. She said she had been lucky and had not seen any Thai fishing boats. Boy! What a relief when I heard her say that.

A month later, my two cousins acquired airplane tickets to the United States. I was very upset that I did not have one yet. But later on, after staying for three more months, I, my sister, and my brother all got tickets and we all came to the United States together.

When we arrived at Bradley Airport in Hartford, my father and my brother were already waiting there to welcome us. After four years away from my father and brother, I thought that they would never recognize us, but I was wrong. When they first spotted us, their eyes were filled with tears. Then Father picked me up and hugged me, which made me feel so emotional that I cried like a baby.

After living with Father for two months, I could not believe how his attitude had changed toward us. He was very gentle and compassionate. I guess most of this change was due to being away from us for so long.

After a year of living with my father, we got a letter from

two of my sisters saying that they had made their escapes and were then in Indonesia. I was so happy that I spread this news all over my high school.

The greatest news of all is that two weeks ago my mother and my two other brothers came over through the Orderly Departure Program. We were all excited and happy, especially my father. He asked us all to thank God for the prayer that had been answered.

From Cambodia

PHYRUN KHATH

My Life Structure

THERE were many events in my life that made me the person I am today. In order to share my personal experiences I would like to first describe what happened to me at the age of three when my mother and I had to be separated from each other. This had to do with the kind of illness I had that couldn't be cured by a doctor. I had to move away from my mother in order to live. I was sent to live with my uncle in Phnom Penh.

It all began when my father took me out of the local hospital and sent me to the most famous hospital in the city of Phnom Penh. My father nervously took me there while my mother went home. My mother was very scared because I hadn't been able to eat or sleep. It was then that she went to see the monk who told fortunes and it was he who told my mother we had a "birth conflict." That meant that if my mother and I lived together, one of us would get seriously hurt. This could endanger our lives. My mother learned that if she wanted to see me live, it was necessary to give me away to somebody else. My mother was totally confused. She cried very hard; she loved me very much but she had no choice.

During my stay in the Phnom Penh hospital, after my father had dropped me off, he went to ask a younger brother who lived in Phnom Penh to visit me frequently and take good care of me. My uncle

*The concept of "birth conflict" is common to many countries of Southeast Asia. It is related to the astrologically determined fortune of the mother and her baby's date and time of birth.—Editors

agreed. Three weeks later I felt alive again. I could eat and sleep much better. Soon afterward I was out of the hospital and stayed with my uncle until my father came to take me home. In the meantime, after my father returned home my mother told him that she had gone to see the monk and started to tell him everything about us.

The monk told her that her last baby boy had died of a birth conflict which she had been unaware of. My parents didn't want to take another risk, so after several days they decided to give me up before my life or my mother's was threatened. My parents both agreed. They decided to send my uncle in Phnom Penh a letter. Since my uncle and aunt couldn't have any children, they were very happy to let me live with them. When I was in the hospital for three weeks they came to visit me every single day. After seeing me all the time they both came to love me very much. Since my brother went to the Phnom Penh lycée, he came to our uncle's house to live too. At first, I didn't mind living with them because my brother was there with me. But when he went back to school, I was left home alone with just my uncle and aunt. I cried a lot, asking them to take me back home but they wouldn't do it.

I didn't want to live with them anymore because it was boring. All I heard were the noises of the cars on the streets and all I saw were the big buildings. It was no fun at all but I had no choice. They started buying me lots of toys. I enjoyed playing with them so I forgot all about home. Things got better. My aunt took very good care of me. They loved me like their own son. I always got what I wanted. Since they had no other children to support, they saved a lot of money. They made their living selling jewelry in their own store. Once in a while, when my older brother had his holiday or vacation, he picked me up and we visited my parents in Suayrain. When I saw them I cried and went to hug them. They cried too. They really didn't want me to go back to Phnom Penh; but they forced me to go back with tears. I had no choice.

At the age of five, my uncle sent me to kindergarten. I went there for just one year and when I was six, the Khmer Rouge took over our country. Phnom Penh was seized on April 17, 1975. The Khmer Rouge forced everyone to leave the city within a week. During that big rush, we weren't allowed to visit my parents again. My older brother and uncle wrote them a letter saying not to worry about me because my brother and uncle could take good care of me. For one week we waited for their response. There was no reply, they all disappeared. We had to leave the city. We couldn't wait any longer for the letter. We left.

A street in the Khao I Dang
refugee camp.
Photo by Elaine Kenseth-Abel.

Approximately one week later, the Khmer Rouge captured all of Cambodia. The Khmer Rouge told everyone not to take too many things because when we arrived at our destination they would provide everything equally to everyone. We packed our clothes and food and headed off with the others. There were thousands of people walking out of the cities carrying everything on their heads and shoulders. Some carried their babies in one hand and their suitcases in the other. It was a sad sight. I walked with my brother, my uncle, and aunt to the train station. That was where the Khmer Rouge wanted us to go. After we got there, we waited for the train for about forty-five minutes. The train finally came. Everybody was pushing and shoving to get on. It took us about an hour to board the train. After we got on, we realized that we had lost our uncle and aunt. We tried to call out their names, but it was just too noisy to hear anything. My brother and I looked everywhere around the train, but saw no sign of them. I cried and asked my brother where they went. My brother replied, "Don't worry, we'll meet them after we get off the train. Stop crying and after we get off, I'll buy you some candy." I stopped crying and sat down, staring out my window. From my seat I could see thousands of people still waiting.

Approximately a half hour later, we were in the countryside. It was a gorgeous view from the train. The rice stems were long and green. The ponds were as blue as the color of the sky. There were also beautiful flowers blossoming in these ponds. Finally, we got to the town near Battambang and we were told to get off the train. Everyone was pushing one another. We finally got off and stood to the side to wait for our uncle and aunt. The Khmer Rouge told everybody to move as fast as possible, so we just kept on moving. Suddenly, my brother realized that he had forgotten his suitcase in the train. He told me to wait for him in an empty spot and said that he would be back. I was very small and people kept pushing me, so I kept on moving and moving.

I later realized that my brother told me to wait for him. Now being so far away from him, I didn't see how I could get back to him. There was only one way to go; I was too small to walk the opposite way anyway. I found myself a spot to wait for him. I waited until dark, but he still didn't show up. I tried to call his name, but my voice was not loud enough. Besides, I only knew his nickname.

It was getting darker and darker. I couldn't see anybody else. I decided to leave without him and followed somebody else's footsteps. After a while, most of the people took a rest under a big tree. I didn't know what else to do so I also stopped to rest under the tree. There was nothing to cover me that night. All I had was a pair of sandals, a shirt, and a pair of pants. I didn't have any food either. There were mosquitoes, and the ground was filthy. I was also starved and worried about what had happened to my brother, uncle, and aunt. I was very confused. It took me forever to fall asleep, but finally I did.

When I woke up in the morning, I felt very weak due to being hungry and tired. My body hurt all over from sleeping on the ground and from mosquito bites. I dreaded continuing my journey, but I had to. So far I had had nothing in my stomach. From morning till five o'clock in the afternoon, I walked with others on an empty stomach. When they stopped for the night, I stopped too. During that night, I was very hungry. I saw a woman preparing rice and I stood there watching her cook. When the rice was done, I was still standing there. As she began to eat with her children, I was still watching them. She looked up and stared at me. After a while she put her eyes down and continued her eating. I wanted very much to ask her for some rice, but I didn't know how to say this politely. I then looked down and walked away with an empty stomach.

People were walking toward the country so I started again to follow the others. I hadn't eaten food for one day and one night now. Around four o'clock, everybody stopped and sat again. I stopped and wandered around looking for my brother and uncle and aunt, but still there was no sign of them. My body was very weary from not eating. Suddenly, I saw another woman cooking rice; I sat near her and watched her cook. When it was done, she began to eat with her children. My hands and body were all shaking from starvation. I finally decided to approach her. I kneeled and put my two hands together and bowed to her, asking, "May I please have some rice?" She just looked at me and yelled "NO!" so I begged her again, "May I please have just a little rice?" My hands were still together and my knees were still on the ground. I was bowing to her, and my head was at her feet. She still said "NO! I don't have any rice for you, now get out of here." A couple minutes later, I put my hands down and walked away. I cried and sat on a piece of wood by myself. All of a sudden, a nice old woman came and asked me what happened, why I was crying. I told her that I was hungry and that I had lost everyone—my uncle, aunt, and brother. She wiped my nose and took me to her grandchildren. She gave me some food and I helped her wash the dishes. I stayed with her for a while until one day she ran out of food, and she told me that I had to leave now. I felt so grateful toward her for giving me food. I walked out and thanked her very much for everything she had done for me. After that I felt depressed again. I followed the others on the walk to the camp.

Finally at six o'clock at night we arrived. Everybody stopped. The Khmer Rouge told all of us to stay put. So everybody started cooking. I didn't have to, because I didn't have anything to cook. All day I had drunk water. My stomach was like a balloon, full of water. I was really hungry again, then suddenly I smelled some food from the camp. I followed the smell of the food and it took me to where the Khmer Rouge soldiers lived. They were also having dinner. I very slowly approached them and asked them for some food. After a while, one of the soldiers threw me a few spoons of rice, I thanked him and quickly picked it up and fed myself. I still wasn't quite full. So I watched them eat for a while. After they finished there were some leftovers. They gave the food to me. I ate everything there was, and helped them wash the dishes. After I was full, I went to sleep.

In the morning, I was hungry again and was looking for food. At noon, I again asked the soldiers for food. They started to push me to the ground and they said that I didn't belong with them. Then all of a sudden, a man came in with a jeep, he was the leader of the Khmer Rouge. He stopped the jeep and came over to me and picked me up. He told me not to worry, that he would take good care of me. After he picked me up, he asked me what my name was and what happened to my family. I told him the whole story, and he understood the difficult position that I was in. I could tell that he felt very sorry for me, so he put me in his jeep and drove me to his home. He asked me if I wanted to live with him. I was very surprised and without thinking I said yes. He pulled me toward him and hugged me very affectionately.

His house was not only big, it was also gorgeous. He took me inside and introduced me to his beautiful wife. I put my hands together and bowed to her. Then he took his wife to one of the rooms in the house and about five minutes later they both came back and he left the house. She took me to the bathtub and gave me a good shower. She also liked me very much. After the shower she put me to bed. I fell asleep right away. It was the first good night's sleep I had had in a long time.

The next thing I knew she woke me up to have dinner. After dinner she told me to play outside. I went outside, but I didn't play. I just sat there and thought about my relatives from whom I was separated.

I lived with this couple for four years, until 1979. I then was ten years old. I was taught a lot of important things about protecting myself. They hired people to teach me how to folk dance and showed me how to use a gun. I always sat on the jeep too, unlike others who had to walk and work. They showed me all the stockrooms where they kept their valuables. For four years I didn't have to work or walk on the mud like others; I was treated like a prince. As time went on, I felt more comfortable living with them so I began to call them "Mom" and "Dad." They told me that they once had a son who looked just like me, but that he died.

In the middle of 1979, since he was the leader of the group of Khmer Rouge, my foster father knew when the Vietnamese were going to invade Cambodia. He told his wife to pack, and he told me that I couldn't go with him because he was a bad guy. If they were caught they would be killed immediately and they didn't want me to die because I was too young to die. Before he left, he gave me the keys to the stockroom and they both hugged me and walked out. The girl that they hired to take care of me asked me to show her where all the valuable things were kept. I took her there and she took many of the things. She told me that she would take care of me, but after she took almost all the valuable things she left without me. I was on my own once again. Luckily, I brought a lot of gold with me from the stockroom. Whenever I was hungry, I took the gold and traded it for food. I was doing all right until one day a young boy came to me, and the two of us became friends. After he found out that I had a lot of gold in my backpack he pushed me down on the ground and grabbed my bag of gold and ran away. I couldn't catch him because he was too fast.

I thought, "There goes my life again." I felt very depressed and lonely and I had nothing left to trade for food. I went hungry for days for I didn't know how to steal. I couldn't ask other people for food because they didn't have a lot either. One day I was crying and an old woman came to me and took me to a foster home. I lived and worked there for a while. One time a young monk went to the foster home and saw me working very hard. He felt sorry for me so he asked one of the women who worked in the foster home if I could go with him and live in the temple. He gave me a schedule of when I should clean and when I could eat. I was very excited. I didn't really care what I had to do as long as there was some food in my stomach. A week later I was working very hard, and he shaved my head and I became a novice. As time went on, I got to like him a lot and he really liked me too. I began to call him "Uncle." After a few months inside the temple there was something wrong, everyone started to leave and I didn't know what to do.

Before he ran away from the temple, the monk took me to his sister and told her that there was something really special about me. He told her to adopt me no matter what happens. So she and her husband agreed to let me live with them. Her family wasn't rich; they made their living by trading gold for rice and they also made some pastries and sold them. From then on I helped them make some money by helping the husband with butchering of animals.

One day we saw a Red Cross van. They announced that whoever wanted to go to the border of Thailand should get in the van. We ran home, packed, and went with the Red Cross van. When we got to the border of Thailand, the woman that I lived with had some gold so she took it and traded it for Thai money to buy food. We stayed at the Thai border for a week and a half. After that she still had some gold left, so she paid some men to take us to Khao I Dang camp. We lived there for at least a year. Things at Khao I Dang camp were much better because food and clothing were provided. During that time, the woman's husband worked for a company next to the Khao I Dang camp hospital and he heard that people could be sponsored to go to America even if they didn't have any relatives living in America. He applied to go to America at the end of 1980. A few months later we received a letter that we were accepted to go to America by our sponsor, the Congregational Church at Williamsburg, Massachusetts. Even though we were accepted, the paper work took quite a long time to complete. In the meantime, the American Red Cross shipped the people who were accepted for America to Singapore. We took a boat to Indonesia and lived there for about a year. During that time I began to call the couple I had been living with "Mom" and "Dad," and their daughter "Sister." Dad went to school to learn some English and Mom stayed home and did the housework. I went to a class where we did singing and dancing. In Indonesia food was provided. We didn't eat all of the canned food so we traded it for other things. Life there wasn't that bad for us.

At the beginning of 1981 the paper work was done. We took a boat back to Singapore and stayed there for about two days. We

Khmer classical dancers give a performance at the Cambodian New Year celebration. (Bowker Auditorium, University of Massachusetts, Amherst).
Photo by Stan Sherer.

then got on a plane for Los Angeles. I was really amazed at the view from the plane thousands of feet in the air. We stayed in a hotel for another two days and then we went to Northampton, Massachusetts. We were placed there because the public housing was much cheaper than regular housing. When I first got to the United States I was really surprised to see all the cars and the big bright buildings.

On September 1982 I began school. I was put in third grade. During that year, I learned how to count from one to ten and how to write from A to Z, and I learned how to write my name. The next year (I was fifteen years old) I entered the ninth grade and continued my education.

If it wasn't for my foster parents who adopted me in 1979, I wouldn't be living in this wonderful country and receiving a good education. I am very proud of myself and of having foster parents to replace my real parents. They treat me very well, with care. They are sending me to college to get a good education. I love them and my sisters very much!

But, of course, sometimes when I think of my real parents I feel very sad and want to cry. They gave me away to save my life. I often think about them and wonder what they are doing now and whether they are all dead or still alive. When I go to my friend's house and see my friend kiss and hug his parents, they all look so happy and proud of one another. I look very sad, and feel guilty and ashamed of myself. I was born from my mother's stomach and I don't even know who my mother really is. Sometimes I feel proud of myself that I survived, and other times I feel very down and depressed because I miss my parents. You always know foster parents are very different from real parents. Every time I talk about my real parents I begin to cry, because it hurts me inside. I know that there is no chance for me to meet them again because I was only a little child when I was separated. Still, I just hope that they are all alive, including my older brother, uncle, and aunt whom I last saw in 1975. This is my life from my birth until now.

ROEUN CHEA

My Unforgettable Experiences

My name is Roeun Chea. I was born in Takeo, a small town in Cambodia, on January 10, 1968. I lived in a one-story medium-sized house which was covered with clay shingles. The floors and the walls were covered with wood. The house was surrounded by a few coconut and palm trees. Next to the house there was a small playground. My home was a peaceful one with a friendly welcoming atmosphere that I shared with my family.

My father, Chea Phon, was thirty-six years old when he died in 1974. He was also born in Takeo, Cambodia. He was a farmer all his life and owned a lot of land and animals. My father was a hard-working man, especially during the rainy season. In addition to growing rice, he also had sugar cane fields and grew corn. In his spare time he went to the river to catch fish for the family to eat. During the dry season my father traveled from town to town in order to sell the rice and corn he had grown. After selling the products he gave the money to my mother to take care of the family. My father was the head of my family and we respected him immensely.

My mother, Sue Thoy, is now forty-nine years old. She usually stayed home to take care of my sisters and me. Once in a while she would help my father in the rice fields. In her spare time she worked as a merchant, buying gold and silver from dealers in Kampong Som and selling it to clients in Phnom Penh. After my father's death, my mother accepted full responsibility for her children and made sure that they had enough food to eat and clothes to wear.

I had four older sisters. Chea Thim was nine years old when she was killed in an air raid during the civil war between the Khmer Rouge and the Lon Nol government at the end of 1974. I now have three sisters. Chea Phat is now twenty-seven, Chea Thoum is twenty-five, and Chea Thai is twenty-two. They are now all married and have children. All three of my sisters and their families are living in Cambodia. My two older sisters helped my father in the rice fields, while the other one went to school. Occasionally when my mother was out on business, my two older sisters stayed at home and took care of me.

In 1974, my father became very sick. He died from malaria in April. My father had worked very hard for his family. He cared more for us than for his own life. After his death, poverty threatened my family. My sisters and I had to help my mother take care of our property.

In 1975, when I was seven years old, I was separated from my family and was sent to live in a children's work camp. One month after I was taken away, they separated all my sisters from my mother and put them in work camps. Finally, they took all of our property, forcing my mother to leave the house and live in a work camp. I lived in the Slang Koung camp for four years. Within the camp, there were strict rules and inflexible routines that everyone followed. The routine started at six o'clock in the morning when it was still dark outside, and the fog was still thick in the air. In the front yard, the ground was wet from dew and the air was cool. I and the other children in the camp would be awakened by the sound of the Khmer Rouge's bell ringing. Although I had not gotten enough sleep, I had no choice but to get up. If I did not wake up, the Khmer Rouge would punish me by depriving me of lunch or dinner. As soon as I heard the bell, I rushed from my bed on the floor and searched frantically for my clothes. Next, I quickly gathered my belongings such as hoe and shovel and put them beside my bed so I could get to them quickly. Then I would comb my hair and brush my teeth. We were never allowed much time for getting ready. After this, I was directed to go outside the house at 6:10 A.M.

Outside in the front yard, I would yawn while waiting for the other children who had not come out yet. Although the day was just beginning, I already felt exhausted by all the jobs I had to do during the day. I wondered why the Communists had to train me this way. I was afraid of them. Later, when all the children had come out of the house, we stood in a line. The line had to be straight and we had to stand properly. In order to do that, we had to extend our left arm fully, and put our left hand on the left shoulder of the person in front of us. After the line was neatly organized, the leader of the Khmer Rouge soldiers began to count the children by calling out their names. If there was one child who had not shown up, they would immediately look for him. Usually the missing child was hiding in a corner to try and get some extra sleep. When the soldiers found him, they would drag the child out of the house.

After we were all there, the soldiers began the meeting. During this ten to twenty minute meeting, the Khmer Rouge soldiers explained to us how the jobs should be done and what they expected. For example, they usually assigned me to work in the rice fields pulling weeds. Five other children would be assigned to work with the dams that kept the water in the rice field. After jobs were assigned to everybody, the Khmer Rouge soldiers asked if we had any questions before doing the work. Then they gave us equipment and at about 6:25 A.M. we started toward our assigned job. Walking to my working place took about forty-five minutes and I started working in the rice field at about 7 A.M. I pulled weeds around the rice plants by hand. Then I used my spade to dig the soil around the plants before taking on another job, for instance, trimming small bushes at the edges of the farm. This trimming was tedious, but I could not complain because I was afraid of the Khmer Rouge soldiers who would wander around the fields to make sure we were working.

Sometimes, I was switched to work on even more difficult jobs, like cutting the weeds and clearing the marsh. To do this, I had to walk into the marsh with my bare feet and trim the weeds. Sometimes the marshy water caused my skin to itch. I scratched and scratched and the itchy area would become infected. While working, I was very hungry because I had no breakfast. We were not allowed to eat anything until lunch, which was served at 12:00.

At 12:15 the Khmer Rouge soldiers brought lunch out to the fields and gave it to the children. Each child received only a bowl of rice soup for lunch. The soup had no taste, no flavor, no nutrition; it contained only a half cup of rice and a bowl of water. One reason why the children were fed this way was because the Khmer Rouge wanted us to learn how to be patient like them. During the war the Khmer Rouge soldiers never complained when they did not have enough to eat. Therefore, they wanted the young children to learn how to be strong and stoic like them and to appreciate how difficult it was during the war. Since they did not feed the children breakfast, there was plenty of food for the soldiers.

I was very sick a few times at work with a headache and fever. I would often fall down because I had not gotten enough rest. I had no medicine to take care of my illness. I thought that I was going to die because many of my friends did die at the working place because they had been physically abused by the soldiers. My life in the camp was very scary and hard to cope with. Sometimes when I woke up in the early morning, I thought of my best friends whom the Khmer Rouge had taken to the forest and killed although they had not done anything wrong. At night I was scared because I was afraid that the Khmer Rouge might take me next.

In January 1979 the Vietnamese occupied part of Cambodia. My home town was totally destroyed by the Vietnamese and Khmer Rouge bombardment, shelling, and shooting. I was terrified seeing all of the shooting and killing that occurred. Two of my friends and I decided to escape from both the Vietnamese occupation and the horror of the Khmer Rouge. Our journey from Takeo to Battambang took us approximately two months by foot. During the journey inside Cambodia, I was exhausted because I had very little to eat and we had to walk all the time. Our living conditions were extremely poor. The road was covered with dust, mud, and pot holes. The houses along the road were torn apart and burned by the Vietnamese air raids. I stayed in Battambang for one month. Finally the Vietnamese government controlled almost all of Cambodia. I had no place to hide from the Vietnamese, so my friends and I decided to escape to Thailand.

Our journey from Cambodia to Thailand took me about one month by foot. It was very difficult for me to reach the Thai border because there were a lot of mountains between Cambodia and Thailand. During our journey, I saw many horrible things that were difficult to accept. Hundreds of Cambodians had been killed by Vietnamese bombs or had died of starvation or sickness. I remember that my two friends stood at the river bank while I crossed the river on a small raft. The raft could not hold more than one person at a time because it was too small. When I reached the other side of the river bank, I saw my two friends and other people there shot to death by Vietnamese soldiers. They died at the scene. After this happened, I traveled by myself along with other people who survived the shooting. In addition, I saw many young babies abandoned by their parents because they could not find food for them. I felt extremely sorry for my people and for my country, especially for the young babies who were just beginning life and found themselves in this world. Unfortunately, there was nothing I could do or say to help them. I would sometimes hold them for a little while and then put them back where I had found them.

During my journey, I was very skinny because I did not have enough food. All I ate was a little bit of rice and edible leaves from the trees. I was bitten many times by insects. The clothes I owned were also unfit for such a journey. For instance, I had only one or two shirts, and two pairs of pants to wear. Moreover, I had no shelter on the way to Thailand, and the weather was very dangerous because it rained and stormed almost every night. Because of this poor weather it was hard for me to find a place to cook.

I finally got to a camp in Thailand. I was very happy because I was safe. I felt as if I had a new life. I stayed in the Khao I Dang refugee camp for almost three years. While I was in the camp, I started to go to school to learn how to read and write in my own native language. I had not had any schooling because of the war. The school buildings in Khao I Dang were made of bamboo tree and palm leaves. There were about six to seven hundred students in each school. In school we divided into two sections. One was in the morning and the other was in the afternoon. Each classroom usually had twenty-five to thirty students. My classes started at 8:00 and lasted until 4:00.

Khao I Dang camp was organized in 1979 by the United Nations High Commission for Refugees (UNHCR) to help refugees who had escaped from Vietnam and the Khmer Rouge Communist regime. In the camp there were many nationalities in addition to Cambodians and Vietnamese. As a refugee, I was faced with many obstacles. There were economic problems and poor living conditions. Living in the Khao I Dang camp was an unforgettable experience for me.

In the Khao I Dang camp, the poor economy caused major problems for the refugees. There were particularly problems with food, water, and clothing. Food was distributed to sections in the camp by the Thai government, and then the leaders of local sections would distribute it to the families. Each month the government would provide every family with a small amount of rice. I received seven kilograms of rice a month. Unfortunately, that was not enough rice for me. If I ate more than the amount I was given, I would not have any rice left at the end of the month. So I had to minimize my eating. Some Cambodian families had to trade their jewelry for rice with Thai people who lived near the camps. Refugees did this because they ran out of food before the end of the month. The people who worked for the Thai government or in the hospitals were fortunate because they were provided with plenty of rice and water.

Water was another major problem for the refugees. It also was provided through the local sections. Each person had five buckets of water a week. Five buckets were not enough for cleaning clothes and dishes and for showering, with enough left over for cooking and drinking. Families who had a lot of children needed extra water for bathing. Because of the lack of water, many children were unclean and would become sick.

Clothing was also distributed by the United Nations High Commission for Refugees to the section leaders. Then the section leaders distributed it to the individual families. The clothes provided by the section leaders were in poor condition. They only lasted for a short period of time, usually about three months, because of the cheap material. Despite the cheapness of the clothes some people still did not have enough shirts or pants to wear. They would wear the old clothes even though they were torn. While I lived in the refugee camp, I had only three or four pairs of pants and shirts and I wore them until they were torn to pieces.

Housing was another major problem. The houses were made of bamboo. Inside the house, there was one room that served as the bedroom and the living room with only one shelf for cooking. The floors were made of bamboo. The walls and roof were made of palm leaves and bamboo straps. If the wind hit my house, the whole thing would fall apart. When the rainy season came, the palm leaves and bamboo straps could not hold the heavy water. Not only did the roof leak, but the walls did as well. One night, for example, everything in my house was completely soaked by the rain. My clothes and my whole body was wet. I was cold because I had nothing to change into so I wore the same clothes at night. I was very scared by the thunder. My heart would pound when I saw lightning in the sky. I was so frightened that I could not sleep all night.

During my time in the Khao I Dang camp, the resettlement officers interviewed me. They asked me about my family in Cambodia and which country I would like to live in. I told them that I would like to go to America. Every time that I think about this country, I think of it as a prize of the world. I wanted to come to America because I was sick and tired of the war. After my interview, they took my picture and sent it to the Lutheran Services in Amherst, Massachusetts. The Lutheran workers took my picture with them and asked American families if they would like to adopt a foster child. They finally found foster parents for me. I was very happy. There was nothing like it.

On May 18, 1982, I flew to the United States through arrangements with the United Nations High Commission for Refugees. First I flew from Bangkok to London and then from London to the United States. My trip took many hours. It was a very beautiful morning, a bright sunny day when my plane took off from Bangkok. While I was in the plane, I was nervous because I had never seen a plane as big as it before. On the other hand, I was excited by the trip. There were many different kinds of nationalities who were on the plane with me: Thai, Lao, Vietnamese, Cambodian, and Europeans. When I arrived in London, I was very surprised to see so many different kinds of people. My ears began to pick up different sounds from every direction and my eyes began to see all the different skins. I stayed in London for about thirty minutes and then I flew on to the United States. On my trip to the United States I faced many difficulties. I had no translator. I had problems communicating with the American stewardess because I did not know the language. Also, since I was not used to American food, it was hard for me to eat, but I had no choice because I did not know how to speak English. I tried to eat the food even though I did not like it. I finally reached America late in the evening, landing at Kennedy International Airport in New York. I had no idea where to go. I walked off the plane with my name tag on the front of my shirt. As soon as I got off the plane, an American man who worked for the refugee people came to me and introduced himself. I was very happy to see someone taking care of me. I stayed at the airport in New York for about thirty minutes and then I took another flight to Hartford. I arrived at Bradley International Airport in Connecticut around noon. I was very excited when I got off the plane. A translator introduced me to my foster family. I felt extremely happy to be in America. I felt as if I had a new life. I was very surprised to see all the new things that I had never seen before, different nationalities and a different environment. After I got my suitcases, we drove to my sponsors' house. On the way I noticed the tall buildings, the cars, and the large highways. Along with my excitement, I felt very lonely because I did not know how to speak the language. All I knew was "yes, no, hello, how are you," which I had learned from the camp. When I arrived at my new house in Amherst, Massachusetts, my parents showed me where my room and the bathroom were located. I was very happy to have a comfortable bed, but even though my bed was very comfortable, I could not sleep well for the first two weeks because I was not used to that kind of bed. In addition, the weather and time were different from Cambodia.

Food was the biggest problem. Since my foster mother is a caterer, she knew what kind of food I usually ate. Most of the time, she cooked Cambodian food for me. I was surprised that she knew how to cook this. After a while, I grew accustomed to eating American food.

Clothing was the only thing that presented no difficulties. Every morning my foster sister prepared clothes for me. She put them near my door. I was pleased with her generosity. Without her I would have had a lot of problems because I did not know American customs.

American culture and society confused me, because there are many different kinds of people living in this country. I had a hard time adjusting to American culture and society. It took me two years to adapt to this environment. I learned from school and from my foster parents.

In June 1982, I enrolled in the ninth grade at Amherst Junior High School. I was very surprised by both the rules and the students. I had trouble with my school work because I did not speak English. While attending school there, I was placed in an English as a Second Language course. I felt uncomfortable because I did not understand the subject material. After a few weeks, I was motivated to catch up on my school work. I always carried a Khmer-English dictionary with me and tried to learn new words every day.

Even though I did not speak English well, I had many friends in school. My classmates were very helpful. They explained the meaning of words and phrases that I did not understand, and as time went by, I felt better about my ability to communicate with my classmates and friends. My English gradually improved and I learned many things about the American way of life.

After living two years with foster parents, I decided to write a letter to Cambodia to find out about my family. I had not seen them since we were separated by the Khmer Rouge. Five months later I received a letter from my mother with photographs. I was very emotional and happy to find that she was still alive. In her letter, she doubted that I was her son because she heard that he had been killed by the Khmer Rouge. She wanted me to prove to her that I was her son, which was difficult because I did not know much about my family background. I wrote her that I had a sister who was killed by the air raid during the war between the Khmer Rouge and the Lon Nol government. When she received that letter, she believed that I was her son. After finally finding my family in 1984, I spent so much time thinking and worrying about them that my school work suffered. In the future, I hope that when my country settles down, I will be able to go back to visit my family; I would like to bring them to the United States.

Now I am living with my foster parents. There are seven people in my family. I have two Cambodian foster brothers. One came to America in 1983 and the other came in 1987. They are still in Amherst High School. I have one American foster brother, who is twenty-five years old, and who graduated from the University of Massachusetts. I have one American foster sister, who is twenty-two years old and who graduated from Tufts University. My father is forty-eight years old. He graduated from the Massachusetts Institute of Technology as a plastics engineer. My mother is forty-seven years old and graduated from Columbia University.

I very much enjoy living with my foster parents. I feel very close to my family. They love me as if I were their real son. They support me in a lot of things, especially my education. Moreover, they help me with my family in Cambodia as much as possible.

Having lived under the dictatorship in Cambodia, I am left with many painful memories. I feel sad and angry because many of my best friends died in the children's camp. I also have emotional problems because I was hurt by living far away from my parents and relatives. I still have bad dreams about my horrible escape from Cambodia to Thailand. As a result of the strictness of the Khmer Rouge rule, I hate the Communist system because of all the jobs that the Khmer Rouge forced on the children. I hope that in the future, I will never have to live under the Khmer Rouge regime again.

Because of my childhood in the Khao I Dang camp, I understand more about life and different environments. I learned to live in a small bamboo shelter and I learned how to make the most of the materials that the Thai government distributed to me. Living in the refugee camp was an incredible learning experience.

After I lived in the United States for several years, my life was filled with learning and an understanding of the new world in which I found myself. I had to face many obstacles in order to succeed. I am proud to be here after adapting successfully to American culture.

In the future, I would like to become a musician and form my own band. I would use the money I earn from my band to help others in poor countries around the world.

BORETH SUN

My Personal Experience

THE civil war in Cambodia began in 1970, when I was five years old. My family was a big one. There were nine people, three brothers, three sisters, my parents, and myself. My family lived in a comfortable house in Battambang, which is one of the provinces in Cambodia. My father, Seth Sun, and my mother, Choeun Chuth, worked very hard to provide my brothers, my sisters, and me with a good life. They tried to give us the best of everything, especially a good education. My father was a businessman and my mother was a homemaker. My father expected us to get a good education, but unfortunately we could not because of the horrible war that caused us untold trouble.

When young, I was known as the "trouble maker" in my family. I attended school for about four years until it was closed due to the war. This war not only devastated the whole country but it also destroyed my family and that of many others.

On March 18, 1970, the former king of Cambodia, Norodom Sihanouk, was overthrown by one of his generals, Lon Nol, with the help of the Central Intelligence Agency. The destruction of Cambodia began when the Americans brought the war from Vietnam into Cambodia. In 1973 the American air force B-52's secretly bombed Cambodia for about seven months causing major damage to the civilian population. The war between the Lon Nol regime and the Cambodian Communists known as the Khmer Rouge lasted for about five years.

After much brutal fighting, the war was finally over on April 17, 1975. The new regime was formed with Pol Pot as the head of the state.

Three days after the victorious Khmer Rouge came into power, they began evacuating the whole population from all towns and the capital city, Phnom Penh. Everyone was informed that the evacuation was only temporary and that it was done to move people to a safe area to protect them from being killed by the American bombing. We believed this and thought that soon we would all return home. But the story was not true. We never returned home and we were forced to live in cooperative camps where families, including my own, were separated.

It was late 1975 when I was separated from my family and taken to live in the children's labor camp. Most of my family members were educated. Under the Khmer Rouge we lived miserably and tragically. My family was horrified, but we could do nothing. We experienced only despair and hopelessness. We were starving to death. This was the first time in my life that I was forced to go to work every day. We were heavily guarded by the Khmer Rouge. All my brothers and sisters were taken away as well and sent to different locations. Only my youngest sister and my parents were together in the same village. I have never seen them since. I have heard that my father was sent to a concentration camp which the Khmer Rouge called a reformatory. He was forced to pull plows and do other hard labor. He got nothing to eat and died because of the punishment.

The Khmer Rouge planned to eliminate all intellectuals. They began to arrest all educated people such as doctors, professors, engineers, and anybody who had connections with the former regime. Then they put these people in concentration camps where they were tortured and executed. At first a lot of people identified their former positions because they were told that if they identified themselves, they would be allowed to work in the fields. When people began to realize that the Khmer Rouge were lying they started to hide their identities. Separating children from parents was an alternative way of discovering people's identities. A lot of children were asked about their parents and, of course, most children told them the truth for they were very innocent and did not know that anything would happen to their parents. Most of the time when one person in the family was found "guilty," the whole family was "guilty."

When I was in a children's labor camp I was forced to work in the rice fields every day. At night, we were "educated" about the

Khmer Rouge's revolution and the regime. Children, including me, who had never worked so hard before had a difficult time adjusting to this situation. A lot of children died because of starvation and the severe punishment from the Khmer Rouge. Our lives daily got worse. The less food we got, the harder we had to work. The Khmer Rouge led us into believing that if we worked harder we would have enough food to eat. This was another lie that the Khmer Rouge told to the people. In addition, in teaching children about the regime the Khmer Rouge also taught children to criticize each other and report each other's faults. All bonds of trust and communication between children were thus broken. In fact, most children who tried to go "home" or broke any rules were taken away and never seen again. Almost all of my close friends died. One time during work, I saw a crab and tried to catch it. When the camp leader saw me he tried to cut my hand off but luckily only my middle finger was chopped off.

During the time of the Khmer Rouge regime approximately three million Cambodians died. I also lost some members of my family. Sometime in 1976, my second oldest brother was arrested and taken away to prison where he was tortured and killed. I saw him before he died. The Khmer Rouge cut his knees, ankles, and the skin on his feet to cripple him so that he could not escape, but he did escape and saw me. Then the Khmer Rouge killed him. The Khmer Rouge soldier who shot him had been his friend. After he was killed, they killed his wife and their only child, a baby. It was later that year that my father was taken away and died as a result of the treatment he received. At this time I was very depressed and emotionally sick. I could not do anything except continue working for the Khmer Rouge and pretend that nothing had happened.

I was in the children's labor camp for a long time and was not allowed to see my family at all. I saw them only once after our separation and then I lost complete contact with them. I've never seen them again. I was moved from one place to another very often. Most of my friends died and later on I escaped and went to join the adult labor camp. Almost everywhere I went, people were dying. In one village I saw all the people had died except one old man; maybe he was a young man but he was so torn that he looked like an old man. He could not walk and was surrounded by the dead of his family. Nobody had buried them. They were left to rot and that man just waited there to die too. There were a lot of bodies scattered around the village. Animals, especially wolves, ate those bodies. The Khmer Rouge did not care whatsoever about the people. All they did was force people to work and try to find faults so that they could kill them. People were powerless to protest against them. Anybody who tried to criticize them ended up dead. The cruel Khmer Rouge had no mercy on any person. They killed and killed.

Sometime in 1978 I escaped with a lot of families, including my aunt's family and my two older sisters, to live in the jungle. In the jungle we lived in the open without any shelter. We moved around often so that the Khmer Rouge would not be able to track us. Living without shelter was very difficult particularly when it rained. We had to make fires most nights because it was cold. Every time it rained, the children cried a lot because they were wet and cold. Even under dense leaves, the raindrops still came through. The major problem in the jungle was food. It was very hard to find food because all the areas of food stores were controlled by the Khmer Rouge. Therefore, we spent a lot of time hunting. We ate leaves as our vegetables. When we got meat we soaked it in ash for a while before we cooked it because we did not have any salt. From 1975 to 1979, hundreds of thousands of people were killed, including the rest of my family. This is the horror of the Khmer Rouge soldiers who killed their own countrymen. The Khmer Rouge controlled Cambodia for almost four years. Then the Vietnamese Communists invaded Cambodia.

I lived in the jungle for a few months until my two sisters and my aunt's family were captured by the Khmer Rouge. I was the only one who was able to escape. Unfortunately, after escaping from the jungle, the Vietnamese soldiers arrested me. This happened in 1979 when the Vietnamese invaded Cambodia. Before my arrest by the Vietnamese, I knew vaguely about the Vietnamese invasion of Cambodia. I was shocked to know that Cambodia was invaded by Vietnamese. The reason that I was arrested was because I was alone without any family and they thought that I was a Khmer Rouge soldier. I was put in a Vietnamese prison for about four days; I was released when they could not get any information out of me. For four days in the prison I was interrogated with the same questions every day. But I told them the same thing every time they asked. That is why I was released so soon. During the Vietnamese invasion, even more people were killed. At that time I became mentally ill. Because I could not find my family, I dreamed about them and felt nothing but fear in the hopeless world. This was the most violent experience I had ever had. Life had become a nightmare for

Rice remains a food staple in Massachusetts and is purchased in bulk. Photo by Sam Pettengill.

me. I was a small boy who struggled to survive through this terrible experience. In 1979 I decided to escape from my country without knowing my destination or fate. Fortunately I escaped from my country and went to live in the Thai refugee camps.

After leaving the prison I did go back to my hometown to try to find my family, but I could not find anybody I knew. It was then that I decided to come to the border camp with a lot of other people. I lived at the border camp for a few weeks, then I went to live in the orphanage in the Thai refugee camp. This is where I started my education again after missing schooling for about six years. I again learned to read and to write in my own language. I lived in the refugee camp for about two and a half years, then I was accepted to come to America. I was sponsored by the Lutheran Service through the Unaccompanied Minors Program in Amherst, Massachusetts. In the Thai camps I felt lost because I was parentless and uneducated. Even so, I struggled to overcome these obstacles, safe from soldiers. I had enough food and had an opportunity to go to school again. I was very curious and ambitious to learn new things. I also was waiting for permission to leave the camp and go abroad. It was 1982 when I was accepted to go to the United States. I was very enthusiastic because I thought I would achieve my goals and at least have a chance for a hopeful future.

At first living with my American family was very difficult. I could not speak English and I had to learn to adjust to the way of life of an American family. I had to attend school again. During my first year in the United States, I was very confused about all the changes in my life: I had to learn English, I had joined a new family, I had started high school and I had to learn American ways. Though at first I could barely speak English, I did well in school after much struggle and determination. I work hard to receive the full benefit of my education.

I am now doing very well and I enjoy living here a lot. In college I am majoring in human services. I hope that the Vietnamese troops will withdraw from Cambodia and that the Cambodian people will live in peace. I also hope that some day I will be able to see my country again.

CHANTHOUK ROS

My Life in Cambodia and the United States

DURING the regime of Pol Pot my family suffered. The Khmer Rouge who were Pol Pot's followers separated us. In July 1976, we were forced to leave Battambang, the second largest city in Cambodia for the countryside. There, the Khmer Rouge separated me and my younger brother (who was five years old) from my parents. At that time I was eight years old. My brother and I lived in the same camp with my third sister. The reason the Khmer Rouge separated Cambodian families was because they wanted people to work in different situations. They placed children five to fifteen in one place. These kids had to do work like picking grass from the rice fields and carrying rocks from one place to another. On the other hand, the young adults of sixteen and over lived in a different camp. Married couples also lived in different places. For these people, the work was harder than that the children had to do. They had to carry logs and work in factories.

Every morning all of the children had to wake at 5:00 A.M. to go to work in the rice fields until 5:00 P.M. Can you imagine how hard it was for young kids like my brother and me to work twelve hours a day and eat only a little food? Every single day we went to work. We were tired and always hungry. We didn't have shoes to wear. As a result our feet were sore and itchy. There were plenty of thorns on the paths and it was very hard to walk with bare feet. Many people caught diseases because they weren't wearing shoes. There was no medicine for curing diseases related to the feet. I always cried when I went to bed at night because I was hungry and exhausted. I also missed my parents. I badly wanted to go home but I could only do that if the leader of the camp gave me a permission slip. The slip certified that I was allowed to go home. I couldn't stay in my camp without seeing my parents, therefore, I left without anyone knowing. When I got home, I found that my parents were very thin because they were working very hard and eating very little. My mother was upset when she found out that the village chief wouldn't let me have any food, so she shared the small amount she had with me. I felt very bad because I couldn't stay with my parents for even one full day. I left my house and returned to my camp. When I got there I was punished because I went home without permission. The leader of the camp forced me to work longer than usual, until late at night, without eating.

At the beginning of 1977, the amount of food that Khmer Rouge provided us was getting even less. Later, they said that they didn't have any more rice. We were given chaff, which is usually for animals. Since we were only eating chaff, we didn't have the energy to work as hard as they wanted us to. I began to get sick and was unable to go to work. The leader of the camp said that people could have food only if they worked. If you didn't work, you didn't eat. At that time, I didn't dare to quit working, so I still went to work while I was sick until I fell down. Then the leader of the camp brought me back. Since I had worked so hard, my sickness had become more serious. I couldn't walk, and was not able to go to work. My meals were reduced. When my friend heard that, she secretly sent a message to my parents. After they learned what had happened, they were very worried because they didn't think I would survive until the time they could get to see me. Therefore, my parents went to ask the leader to let me stay with them and rest for a few days. He agreed, and I was allowed to go home. Five days later, I got better and returned to the camp.

In the middle of 1977, my baby brother (who was two years old) died from hunger. We were very upset to learn that. Moreover, we heard that my mother's sister's family was killed by the Khmer Rouge soldiers because her husband was a member of Lon Nol's army. When we received news that my two sisters were forced to get married, my mother almost became a maniac. When someone wants to marry your daughter, he has to ask your permission first. If the parents agree to let their daughter marry, it won't hurt their feelings. My parents were furious and very hurt when they received that bad news. None of us was satisfied with the wedding ceremony because it was worthless. Before 1975 a wedding always had food and drink for the guests. It was strange to me that when Pol Pot came to power in Cambodia, they didn't have any food for the ceremony. When the couples' families saw them, they quietly cried. During the announcement of the wedding, I knew the seventy-five couples included my two sisters. When each name was called, that couple had to get up and shake hands with pale faces. Then the ceremony was over. Because my mother was worrying about the death of my aunt's family and my brother's death, she became very sick. My sisters and I tried to find a way to come home, but the leader of the camp wouldn't let us visit my mother at all. They said that even if we went to visit her, she would not get better and that we shouldn't waste our time, we should just stay in the camp and keep working harder. We felt very bad when they said that to us. There was nothing we could do except to stay in the camp and cry.

In July 1979, when the Vietnamese took over Cambodia, all my sisters and my brother escaped from the camp to live with our parents. At that time, all my family got back together again. We were very happy, hoping that we would have freedom, and everybody was delighted to be with the family. Months later the Vietnamese government began to treat the Cambodian people more harshly. They started to record all of the property that an individual family owned so that they could tax it. Furthermore, it was hard for people living in the villages because some bad Vietnamese soldiers robbed the people and kidnapped young women. Every night we were very afraid of what might happen. We also ran out of food. There was no way to support our family. We decided to leave our hometown to live on the Cambodia-Thai border.

My family left Cambodia in September 1979. From Battambang to the border, it took eight days of walking. During the trip in the forest, we met people who were passing along the border and had been robbed. It was very scary to hear their stories. We had to get into the camp, however, so we decided to risk our lives in the forest. When we reached the midpoint, the group of people my family and I were traveling with were robbed by a group of Vietnamese. I didn't know whether they were soldiers or not. They raped four girls and took five others with them. On the eighth day of the trip we reached the camp which was called Khao I Dang. This camp on the Thai border was supported by the United Nations and the American Red Cross.

It was very dangerous for people who tried to get into that

camp, because Khao I Dang was surrounded by a metal fence and by Thai soldiers. The Thai soldiers always attempted to shoot at people who were trying to enter the camp. While we were trying to break through the fence, the Thai soldiers saw us. They shot at us. Members of my family were lucky; no one was wounded. There were about a hundred people in the group that was trying to enter the camp. Eight were killed and ten were wounded. About half of the people were arrested, and the other half were able to enter the camp. After the shooting, the soldiers also arrested my family. They then took us to jail. They said that if we wanted to get out of the jail, we would have to pay 1,000 baths in Thai money so that we could stay in the camp. Otherwise, they would take us back to the Cambodian border. We had to find where my aunt lived in order to borrow some money. Finally, we found her. My mother borrowed 6,000 baths. There were six of us so we paid them 6,000 baths. We were very happy to have a chance to live in that camp. While living in the Khao I Dang camp I went to school and worked so that I would have enough money to help my mother to pay back my aunt. Besides going to the Cambodian school, I also went to sewing school. I really tried hard to find a job. At that time, my sisters and my brother also went to a different school. I was the best student in my school. I was elected to be the student president.

From 1982 to the end of 1983 life in Khao I Dang camp was very difficult. Every night there were a lot of robbers. Those robbers were both Thai and Cambodian. Whenever they broke into the camp to rob people, they always raped at least four to six girls. Sometimes they took a few girls with them to live in the jungle. At that time I was sixteen years old, and my sister was eighteen. Every night, we couldn't sleep easily. When we heard the shooting, we tried to hide under the bed. My mother was very worried about both of us. She prayed to God every day that the two of us would not be raped or taken away. It was very hard for us to live like that.

On August 19, 1983, my family was interviewed by the resettlement committee about coming to the United States. We were sponsored by my aunt, who had come here in 1980. We were very pleased to get out of the Khao I Dang camp. I had a feeling that from then on, we would have a happy life in the United States. We left Thailand for the United States on February 19, 1984. It took us four days to go from Thailand to the United States. I was very surprised when

I first got on the airplane, because I had never seen such a big plane before.

On February 24, 1984, my whole family arrived in Boston. We were very happy to see my aunt and her family. We had not seen each other for three years; I was excited to see them. We had all missed each other very much. About a week later, my uncle sent me, my sister, and my brother to Boston High School, which was the first high school I ever went to. The day that I walked into that school, I looked like a dumb person because I didn't know any English. I acted strange compared to the other students and I also looked different from those students who had lived here all their lives. When I was in my country, I used to be quiet and I never talked unless I had something to say. In addition, I was not allowed to go out. Therefore, when I first came to Boston, my personality was different. Most students thought of me as an isolated person, so no one ever wanted to speak with me at all. On the other hand, all my classmates went out to the park or to parties. I never dared to go with them because I was afraid of my parents. At that time, I was very lonely. I had no friends except for my family. I could not stay like that any longer so I decided to ask my parents to give me permission to be with my classmates. My parents finally agreed. From then on, I joined my classmates and became more accepted.

Since I now have a lot of American friends, my attitude has changed. From them I have learned a lot about everything in America. They taught me English pronunciation and spelling. They told me that I have to speak out. They also told me not to be shy when I talk to other people. I always paid attention to what they were saying. I am very appreciative of what my friends taught me about American customs.

HONG TAING

My Best Memories

BEFORE 1975, my family and I lived happily in a big house in Phnom Penh, the capital city of Cambodia. There were eight people in my family—my parents, my two older brothers, my two older sisters and my little sister. My siblings and I went to school and my father went to work as a teacher of mathematics. My mother stayed home and took care of the children and the household. My parents often took my little sister and me to visit the old historic buildings and also wat Phnom. Here many people gathered for the traditional activities on special holidays like the New Year days. We also liked to go to the parks for recreation. These were good times of happiness which I do not forget. We often spent time together—our family talking about the old times and the future. We loved each other very much. I obeyed my parents, brothers, and sisters.

We ate our rice gladly and always set aside some for the monks. They came to our house every morning with their alms bowls. It is part of our Buddhist religion to offer rice to the monks once a day. We believed in Buddhism.

I was very happy and proud of my family. We had a lot of relatives: aunts, uncles, cousins, nieces. There were also good friends who lived near our house.

It was about nine o'clock in the morning of April 17, 1975. I was not quite eight years old. My father and brothers were standing in front of our house greeting the victors, the Khmer Rouge led by Pol Pot. They had fought hard to beat Lon Nol's soldiers. The Khmer Rouge had invaded Phnom Penh. Uncle Sreng and his friends asked my brothers to go with the crowd to congratulate the victors. They walked and ran to follow the Khmer Rouge tank and loudly shouted to cheer them. It was exciting! Even though people had been killed and houses were burned, everyone was very happy because the war was over. We all thought that Cambodia was going to become a peaceful country. My mother brought out mangoes and bananas for the Khmer Rouge soldiers. She was happy, too.

In the afternoon the Pol Pot soldiers told people to surrender their weapons. I saw many guns piled in every street. My brother went to one of those gun piles and put his gun there. He also left his police uniforms on the pile.

The Khmer Rouge told people who lived in Phnom Penh to leave home for a few days so that they could clean up the city. They also said that they were afraid of the American air force dropping bombs on the city. We were now forced to leave Phnom Penh. Everyone left the city to live "temporarily" in the countryside. This didn't include the Khmer Rouge who remained. After people had left Phnom Penh, the streets, hospitals, temples, houses, and schools were very quiet. In fact, the whole city was like a ghost town. The Khmer Rouge had lied to the people when they told them that everyone would be allowed to return to the city after three days. They tried to move people out of the city for ever.

My family and many relatives moved to a small village called Phlow Trey, located near the Mekong. Life was difficult. We had a lot of money but we could not buy anything because the old money was no good during Pol Pot's regime. My parents were very discouraged. They could not say a word. They became silent. My family had to build a hut out of bamboo and trees.

Three months later, the whole village was moved to another small village, called Doun Tree which was located in Battambang Province. People were expected to help harvest the rice crops. My family and I cried without tears. Angka (the Khmer Rouge directorate) offered us nothing but the little hut in the rice field. There was no water. We had to walk about two miles each day to get to the fields. Life became more difficult!

Everybody had to work very hard, seven days a week,

from sunrise until sunset. It was really sad. We could only see each other at night after work. I was forced to work as a herder. I took water buffalo to the river to let them bathe. I also made sure that the buffalo always had enough grass.

The Khmer Rouge tried to make me answer questions about my family background. My family taught me not to answer when I was asked about my family, so I always said I did not know.

It was almost the end of 1976. The rule of Angka became harder and harder. My brothers and sisters were separated from the family to work in fields that were very far from my parents, who were greatly shocked. They were very upset when they were told. Even though my parents begged the leader not to separate us, he could not let us stay together. He simply said that it was the Angka's decision. Everyone had to obey and believe in Angka. My parents were assigned to work in the cabbage and pumpkin fields from morning until night. They cried and worried a lot about their sons and daughters who had been taken away. My little sister and I were forced to work on road construction in the village. We worked in a group of thirty people digging up dirt to repair the road that had been destroyed. At night, we came back home and had dinner together without my brothers and sisters. I cannot forget it! My little sister and I cried almost every night because there were so many mosquitoes. In fact, we did not have a mosquito net. My parents could not get enough sleep. As a result, they became weaker and weaker. My mother was very sick.

In the year 1978 I was separated from my parents. I had to work and stay in the youth camp which consisted only of young people between twelve and seventeen. I was then twelve years old. The situation in the camp was even harder than in the village. The Khmer Rouge did not let people get enough sleep or enough rice to eat. I ate once a day because that was all I could get. Meals consisted of one cup of rice cooked with or without vegetables—this to feed five to ten people. They were not the meals we were used to. It was like pigs' food! I did not seem like a human being at all, I was so skinny, really thin. I wore old black clothes which were torn. Then I went to dig a canal. Sometimes I had to work at night if they did not have meetings. The meetings were just sitting and listening to the Khmer Rouge talk about how hard we were supposed to work in the fields. They asked people to volunteer to tell Angka about their family background.

One night, I missed my parents so much that I ran away from the camp to see my parents. Around eleven o'clock at night, I had run about half way through the camp when one of the leaders caught me. I was very scared! He took me back and had his vice leader punish me. My hands were tied. They beat me with a bamboo stick again and again. It was very painful but I dared not cry. Instead, I begged them to let me go visit my parents. Although I begged them, they kept saying no. They told me if I dared run away again, I would be killed. I was not given any food to eat for three days, but I was still forced to go to work.

When I told them that I had been very sick, they gave me medicine which was made from the bark of a tree and told me to go to work. There was no hospital. I had to go to work with my sickness in order to be allowed to eat one meal a day. I missed my parents very much. They had never punished me at all.

Two months later, my brothers' and sisters' camps were moved near my camp. These groups worked harder than ours and ate more food than we did. One day, my sister saved her meal for me because I told her that I was very hungry and that I was sick. At night, she brought it to me and then quickly left my camp. I was very happy then and I looked for a quiet place to hide while eating the rice she had brought. Rice! I had not seen enough for more than a year. When I looked around and did not see anybody I opened the rice box and ate. Unfortunately my leader caught me while I was eating.

Here goes my life again! He took me to his leader and told him what I had done. They kicked me while they were questioning me about how I got the rice. I lied to them that I had stolen it in order to save my sister's life. It was true that no one could offer anything to someone else. It was against Angka's rule. No religious belief, no individual love, one had to love Angka.

A month later, my brother was taken away by Angka. He was never released to return to the camp. The reason was that Angka found out about his past occupation in Lon Nol's regime. He had been a police officer in Phnom Penh. He was killed by Pol Pot's soldiers. The Khmer Rouge killed many people: doctors, lawyers, police, teachers, engineers, soldiers, businessmen, and wealthy people.

My parents' past was not discovered, but life in the village was cruel. All old and young people were forced to dig irrigation ditches. My parents were not able to work hard anymore because they were old and did not get enough food to eat. My mother's sickness was getting worse. She died from her illness. My father died of starvation. The Khmer Rouge killed people in many ways. They were obsessed with the act of genocide. Death was everywhere. It was very scary!

The Khmer Rouge destroyed temples and the monks' residences. They did not believe in Buddhism or any other religion. They did not even celebrate the New Year days. They eliminated our old culture and its traditions. They changed the New Year days into their most important meeting days. Everyone had to attend these big meeting days. There the Khmer Rouge forced everyone to answer questions about family background. When the meeting ended, everyone had to go back to where they belonged and go back to work the next day.

In 1979 my family had five people—my brother, my three sisters, and me. Fortunately the Vietnamese soldiers invaded Cambodia. My brother, sisters, and I moved from the village to live in the city of Battambang. Although the Vietnamese came to rescue us from the "killing fields," the living conditions were still difficult. We did not have food because we did not have any gold with which to buy rice. We decided to go to the Thai-Cambodia border in order to live under better conditions. When we arrived at the border we met many Cambodians who came from different places. They came from all over war-torn Cambodia. We stayed there for two months. Then Thai people took all of us to Doung Rek mountain and left us there. We were among a number of people who tried to walk back to Cambodia. Unfortunately many were killed by the mines and bombs or died of hunger. We got back safely to Battambang and decided to live there. My brother and older sisters planted vegetables to trade for rice. My little sister and I happily went back to school. We made friends and studied very hard and helped our brother and sisters on the farm. Hospitals, temples, and other businesses were reopened. My brother decided not to move because he could make his living in Battambang.

In 1982 I asked my brother and sisters to let me leave Cambodia for Thailand because I heard that one could come to America through a special organization. They would not agree to let me so I ran away from home and left a note saying that I was going to Thailand.

I fled Cambodia and the Communist regime that killed my parents. I was very scared when I escaped from Cambodia. I walked through the war zone and the jungles in the dark night. It was very dangerous and I will never forget it. Many people not only lost their belongings, but they were also killed by the mines or died of starvation.

Luckily I passed all of the obstacles safely and found a refugee camp located in Thailand. The camp was called Khao I Dang and was under the United Nations High Commission for Refugees (UNHCR). The camp provided many different kinds of education, such as elementary school, secondary school, and a training school. In the refugee camp I was very excited when I met a family I had known from Cambodia. I asked them whether I could stay temporarily with them and they were very kind. I was so pleased that they let me stay with them. Here I was offered a meal every day by UNHCR and the Red Cross.

While I was waiting to be accepted by the United States resettlement program I attended secondary school and also attended an English-speaking private school.

I was transferred to the Philippines on July 27, 1983. I was put in a new refugee center which was called the Philippines Refugee Processing Center (PRPC). Here I continued attending an English-speaking school and also participated in the International Catholic Migration Commission's intensive assistant teacher training school. When I completed the training program, I worked as an assistant teacher and interpreter in the cultural orientation classes that prepared refugees in the PRPC for entering the United States. My duties included translating the lesson into Cambodian or Cambodian into English and assisting the teacher in the classroom.

I was admitted to the United States in accordance with the Refugee Act of 1982 on March 23, 1984. First, I was sponsored by the Derbyshire Baptist Church and lived in Baltimore, Maryland. Then I moved to Northampton, Massachusetts, to live with my cousins. I attended Northampton High School. I studied very hard to be able to graduate as a student of the class of 1987. I continued successfully learning English and adapting to American culture. While I was studying at Northampton High School I had an after-school job. I worked part time at the Northampton Nursing Home to help support myself. I am now attending the University of Massachusetts as a member of the class of 1991. I am willing to study as hard as possible. A college education and preparation for a professional career are the most important goals in my life.

As a consequence of my having lived under a Communist

regime for many years, with starvation, cruelty, sickness, and death, I have become aware that life under a Communist regime is hard. Such a regime will take away your home, your religion, your education, your relatives, and even your life. Even though I am now living peacefully and happily here in America, I will always have bitter memories of what happened in Cambodia—the bloodshed and tragedy of Cambodians and of my life. I miss my family very much!

MARK GRAY

The Khmer Rouge—Murderers

THIS is a story that my friend Vannorath Sarin told me. Like many other young Khmer people, Vannorath left the Khmer Republic after a period of total chaos. Political and economic strife struck the heart of an already fragile system when the radical Communist group Khmer Rouge took over the capital Phnom Penh on April 17, 1975.

Vann's family's ethnic background is completely Khmer, with the possible exception of a great-grandmother who was Chinese. His family's social and economic background was respectable; his father was a navy captain and his mother was a housewife with a small business on the side. Vann's father attended to naval duties in Kampong Som in the south for four to six months each year while his family remained in Phnom Penh. The rest of the year he was free to spend with his family. Vann's mother tended the household and cared for the children with the help of her four sons and five daughters, of whom Vann was the third oldest son. The business consisted of selling foodstuffs such as sugar in Vietnam, Kampuchea, and Thailand. Business was conducted at the family's convenience and it did not disrupt family life.

Vann was ten years old and attending school in the new year of 1975 when the situation in Kampuchea started to deteriorate. Controlling most of the countryside, the Khmer Rouge began an attack on the capital in April and stormed the city on April 17. Vann's father was at home when the event took place. His mother, however, had been visiting in Kampong Som with her brother, presumably taking care of some business. After the occupation, Vann's mother did not dare return to Phnom Penh, but instead sailed on a boat to Thailand with a place provided by her brother who was a second lieutenant in the navy. The people on the boat had no idea of what was going on in their country while they were away.

Back in the capital, the Khmer Rouge were expelling everyone from the city to the countryside. Those were frightening days of uncertainty for Vann and his family. Since the markets were not in operation, the people in the city were eating what they had stored in the form of canned food and rice.

Through those hours of waiting to see what would happen, the only thing people could do was listen to the radio. However, the media was now controlled by the Khmer Rouge, and they were reporting that the Americans would soon drop bombs on the city because of the Communist takeover. This propaganda was used to compel the people to leave the city. Soldiers were entering homes and forcing people to leave. Vann and his family had less than an hour to pack all they could carry.

The exodus from the city was enormous. Millions of people were ordered to travel by foot to populate the countryside and promote agriculture. No one was exempt. Vann and his family chose to resettle in Takeo, near the eastern border with Vietnam, where his mother's relatives lived.

During his family's stay at Takeo, three of Vann's younger sisters died of disease and malnutrition. Obtaining enough rice from the government authorities was a constant problem and led to many deaths after the Khmer Rouge took over. Even though greater numbers of people were working at rice cultivation, organization was poor and corruption was high.

Eight months after their move to Takeo, Vann's family was ordered to leave and go to Battambang, located in the north, close to the Thai border. It was approximately two years after their arrival in Battambang that the killing ordered by the Khmer Rouge leaders began. The Khmer Rouge soldiers, many of them less than twenty years old, began to persecute, torture, and kill on sight anyone who was suspected of having been remotely connected with the former regime. Intellectuals and military personnel were the particular targets, as were monks and anyone who could be identified as a political figure of the old system.

Vann's father, having been a captain in the national army,

and his oldest brother, who had received a bachelor's degree, were automatically placed in great danger. One day when Vann was tending to some oxen in the field, he returned to learn that the Khmer Rouge had taken his father and brother away and killed them. Another older brother, Denora, was about twenty then and could take adequate care of the children who were left, with the help of an aunt who was living in the same village. Vann's remaining two sisters had died of starvation and disease, so just three brothers remained.

After a total of four years in Battambang, new events altered Vann and his brothers' freedom. The Vietnamese Communists took over the country in early January 1979. It was believed that the Vietnamese invasion was ordered by the Soviet Union, the source of Vietnamese arms, in order to stop the killing and to give them more influence over the area. Although the people were free from Pol Pot's Khmer Rouge, they were not free from the restraints of communism. It is true, however, that after the Vietnamese took control, the Khmer people were allowed much more freedom of movement within the country, repopulating the area around Phnom Penh. Trading in the markets began again.

Vann's aunt entered the profitable business of buying and selling gold and diamonds, thus providing well for the extended family. Vann's brother Denora was asked by the Vietnamese authorities to go to the Soviet Union to take up studies at a university. This prompted him to escape to Thailand with hopes of resettling the entire family in a country free of the turbulence of communism.

Once in Thailand, Denora sent a Cambodian friend to tell Vann and the others that they should come to Thailand where they could make arrangements to go to the United States. They had chosen the United States because their uncle had already immigrated to Holyoke, Massachusetts. His mother also had traveled with their uncle, but she later returned to Kampuchea.

Vann's younger brother and his cousin began their long journey to Thailand by taking a bus from Phnom Penh to Battambang. His aunt had decided to stay behind with some other relatives and continue in her prospering business. From Battambang the boys had to walk through jungles and cross the Thai border. They walked a distance of forty kilometers, starting at four in the morning. The road they traveled on was filled with water and mud, making the way more difficult. There were others trekking that road to reach the border. At one point, Vann asked a man to take his little brother on his bicycle because he could not withstand the trip. Vann and his cousin continued, sure of the roads in Thailand, where they arrived at 6 P.M.

Their first camp was Khao I Dang, where the reunited family spent about one or two years. Next they moved to the Mairut camp, closer to Bangkok, at which they were allowed to visit and enjoy some amusements with the money they had kept or earned from working in the camp. Their stay here was for a period of only three months. Then they went to Transit Chonbury for two days.

Their wait was finally over; their destination was marked for the United States. All but the youngest brother had sponsors in Massachusetts; the youngest had been sponsored by a friend of Vann's father who was living in California. The boy would join the others later. The day for which Vann had been waiting for so long finally came: August 29, 1981.

The newness of the surroundings was amazing at first. Everywhere Vann went the buildings and cars were modern, quite different from the deteriorating society he knew only a few years ago. Although he was sad to have left his mother country, he was very happy to be in his adopted one. He was glad to see American people, with whom he had little contact when he was in Kampuchea.

Vann began high school immediately in September 1981, taking courses in English, math, history, and industrial arts with students who had been speaking English all their lives. He also took an ESL course. He not only fared well in his first year in school, he also surpassed most of the other students. The need to survive proved to be a great motivator.

Socially, Vann felt very uncomfortable at first. He had few friends and the ones he did have often were not able to understand his English. They asked what he was doing in the United States if he didn't know English, and few of them knew anything about his country. At times he felt lonely and depressed and turned toward home for support, where they always understood him.

Since that time in high school, Vann has improved his speaking ability considerably. His desire to find another world in which he can live in freedom has been realized. He now studies at the University of Massachusetts, preparing for a life that will eventually profit future generations of Americanized Asians.

SRENG KOUCH

Despair and Hopelessness

ONE day in the beautiful country of Cambodia, a Chinese man named Kouch Meng married a Chinese woman named Taing Ly. In Chinese, it does not mean that the man was Mr. Meng nor does it mean that the woman was called Mrs. Kouch. No! In America it means Mr. Kouch. My mother keeps her family name—Taing—and we the children take the father's name. Hence I am Sreng Kouch.

My parents were married in 1962, after which they were expected to occupy a section in the Kouch family home, helping with the family business. Since the Kouch family was middle class and well educated, they had no problem with financing; therefore, Taing Ly lived comfortably with her in-laws. A year later, my parents decided to start their own business to build for the future, so my Kouch grandfather gave them a house from the seven houses he had built for his seven children. He also helped establish them in their own business. Both of them sold things in their store. Life for that couple has been beautiful and happy ever since.

On August 25, 1967, I was the first child born to my family. Then things started to change. My father continued his work in the household. Soon a little sister and a little brother came along. There were three of us then and they were expecting more. In my country people love and want many children. I was too young to understand life, but my parents told me that the situation in our family living had remained the same since the three of us were born. Our lives were beautiful. Our country was beautiful.

Then the bad things started to happen. On March 18, 1970, the monarchy fell. Prince Sihanouk left the country and Lon Nol became president. He stepped up the defense of the country against the Communist Khmer Rouge. Men over eighteen were obliged to enlist. Men with the responsibility of large families (my father was one of them) could remain civilians if they paid a considerable sum of money to aid the war effort. My father told me that he hated the Khmer Rouge. He wanted to fight in this civil war, but with three children and my mother pregnant again, he just could not leave us behind. He also told me that the Khmer Rouge did not like rich or intellectual people. They fought to take over this country and set up a new rule so that all citizens could have equal opportunity.

To protect us, my family and I decided to take refuge in a small town, leaving behind our house, business, relatives, and everything that had pointed to a good future. We settled down in Bo Bai Len, a small town near the Thai border, so that if Cambodia fell we could escape to Thailand within a few hours. There my father started a new business and my mother continued to care for the home and the family.

In 1974, the Cambodian government became powerless as the Khmer Rouge came closer and closer to the capital. I was old enough to attend school, but unfortunately I was unable to since they were closed. At last, on April 17, 1975, Pol Pot, a Communist leader, took control of Cambodia. The Communist government forced the people to leave their cities and towns, to abandon their homes and possessions.

Since the Communist takeover was so quick—twenty-four hours—my family had no chance to arrange our affairs. We had no choice but to leave everything we owned behind and again we left our town without knowing our destination.

Five days after a long walk, we ended up in the forests. From that time on our family and others, approximately a hundred families in a newly set-up town, were forced to work day and night. The Communist party was so powerful that they could do whatever they wanted and if any person attempted to fight or disobey them, he or she would be killed. The Khmer Rouge always tried to find fault with innocent people. Soldiers, foreigners, well-educated people, and many upper-class families were executed by the Khmer Rouge on any pretense.

My family had never done such hard labor in our lives. We had always had a good life. Now we were almost starving to death. We worked every day including weekends and holidays without pay. My father worked in the rice field, pulling plows and doing other hard labor. My mother and my little sister worked to clear out the forest and plant corn, bananas, potatoes, and other things. I was nine years old then, and that is when I was taken away from my family. I worked as a cowboy, watching thousands and thousands of cows and water buffalo.

From 1975 to early 1979, millions of people were killed. Most of them starved to death, and some were killed because they disobeyed or disagreed with the Communist party. This is the horror of Khmer killing Khmer for nothing. Fortunately, we survived through these horrible circumstances.

On January 9, 1979, the Vietnamese Communists invaded Cambodia and we were allowed to return to our town. We found that ours and many other houses were burned to the ground. We had no place to stay. We felt nothing but despair and hopelessness about the future. My father told me that the Vietnamese Communists were only pretending to help us, the Cambodian people, and that in reality they were trying to take over our country. Almost a year later we decided to escape from Cambodia, the only way my parents could see for their children to have an opportunity to go to school and to start a new life away from the horror.

It took three days and four nights to escape from Cambodia to a refugee camp in Thailand. On our way, we were robbed by Vietnamese soldiers. Many times we missed stepping on bombs which were set up by the Khmer Rouge. Fortunately, we managed to cross the border and were assigned to the Thailand camp called Khao I Dang.

In Khao I Dang, I was old enough to help my father when he began again to buy and sell things in the camp. We bought and sold things to support our big family. Also we were waiting for permission to leave the camp and go abroad. Finally, on June 29, 1980, we were accepted for immigration to the United States under the sponsorship of the United Methodist Church.

Upon our arrival in the United States, we were lost and confused because we could hardly speak English, but our American sponsors were very friendly and kind to us. They rented a house for us and supplied us with furniture and clothing. They helped my father get a job, and they put us in school. We are very grateful because our dream

A Cambodian family before departure for Amherst, Massachusetts. (Khao I Dang refugee camp).
Photo by Elaine Kenseth-Abel.

had come true. We were alive. We were safe. We were together. We now live in Lynn, Massachusetts. Even though my parents started a new life with nothing but a little help from American friends, they worked very hard to support our family. My father works full time at the West Lynn Creamery as an assembler and my mother works part time at Cruising Design Incorporation in Peabody and takes care of the family. My three sisters, three brothers, and I are all in school.

During my first year in school, I could barely speak English. Even though I started in an English as a Second Language program, I did well in class and the following year I was placed in a regular class with the American students. At Lynn English High School I majored in computer science and mathematics. I have been interested in the computer field since I came to the United States and first heard about it. I worked during the summers at the West Lynn Creamery. In my senior year I applied to the University of Massachusetts, Boston University, and Wentworth Institute. I got accepted by all three of them, but I decided to come to the University of Massachusetts at Amherst. Here I am a student, living on campus in Dwight Hall, and majoring in computer science.

What a long, long way from the Khmer Rouge, war, death, refugee camps. . . . God bless America!

HORNG KOUCH

My Bloody Nightmare

Hi, my name is Horng Kouch. My nationality is Chinese, but I was born in Cambodia. I was born in 1969 and lived happily in a wealthy family until Cambodia's capital was captured by the Khmer Rouge. Then my life was turned upside down. Cambodia became a Communist country and the year 1975 turned into "The Year Zero." I lived like a queen until April 17, 1975. That was when my bloody nightmare began.

There are many events in my life that made me the person I am today. I would like first to describe what happened in Cambodia and how these events affected me and my family during the last thirteen years. We were forced to leave our home, we were separated, starved, enslaved. Finally, in 1979, we fled these horrors, first to a refugee camp in Thailand and from there to Lynn, Massachusetts. In 1975, as a child of six, I had to face many obstacles. I was forced to attend the execution of prisoners in the forest. I'm sure that most American people have never experienced this. My life was like a cloud in the sky, which moved one day here, one day there and sometimes seemed to vanish altogether. My life had no future. I lived only for the day. My family was separated in several different places. I hardly saw my father or my older brother and sister. The Khmer Rouge forced me to work far outside the village. Every day I saw people die of starvation or be murdered. At first, I was really frightened by seeing people die. I always thought that they were killed because they did something wrong to other people, but then I realized that the Khmer Rouge killed people for arbitrary reasons—

perhaps because they were well educated, or ill, or well known. After I found this out, I was even more frightened because my parents were once very well known and wealthy. I was afraid that the Communist leader, Pol Pot, might take them away from me and that I might never see them again. So every day my two younger brothers and I prayed to the Ancestor Spirit to let them live for another day. Unfortunately, my three-year-old baby sister died of illness because there was no medicine to cure her and no time to take good care of her. But we were lucky, nine out of ten of us survived in my family. Every time we think of the baby we cry and call her name. We do this when we pray on special occasions such as the New Year and five or six other times a year. We also make a commemorative celebration for her soul to rest in peace on the date that she passed away. Celebrating the spirit of the dead person is very common in Cambodia.

When I was living in Cambodia nineteen years ago, my parents were very wealthy and well known. They owned two big buildings. We had six maids to help around the house. My parents loved me very much. Therefore, I always got whatever I wanted. It's too bad that I was too young to know and enjoy what I really had. I did not have any education when I was living in Cambodia. By the time I was six and was old enough for school, Cambodia had already fallen to the Communists. That was 1975, the same year when Pol Pot, the new Communist leader and his followers, the Khmer Rouge (Red Khmer) took over our country. They closed all schools. They forced all the Khmer people to move out of the city, and whoever refused was immediately killed. My family and I had to move out of the city and settle down in the "New Economic Zone," in the forest. It felt like everybody in my family was falling apart. I was separated from my family and sent to a camp with other children the same age.

It was strange and very difficult for me to change my life style over such a short period of time. Things that I had never seen or done before, I had to experience. I even had to attend public executions of prisoners! I had to work hard. I had to sleep on the ground using sand as my mattress and a rock or a piece of wood as my pillow. Not only did the food taste bad, there also wasn't enough for everyone. Almost everybody in my family was sent to work. My father was sent far out of the village in the fields cutting rice, carrying it to be threshed, and sometimes making roads for farmers. He was allowed to visit home once or twice every six months. My mother didn't have to work far from home because her children were still very young, so she worked at a job threshing and winnowing rice. She hand plucked the rice from the stems, and sometimes gathered wood for the common mess. Both my older brother and sister were sent away to work. Their jobs were digging dirt to make a dam for a small irrigation pond and making a dike for people to cross the rice fields. These kinds of jobs don't seem very hard but we were working twelve hours a day, seven days a week, including holidays, and some of us got really sick and tired of this work.

Within our family, there were five of us who worked, and two stayed home. My five-year-old brother took care of my three-year-old sister. One day my baby sister had bloody diarrhea and cried a lot. She was ill, but my mother couldn't really take good care of her because she wasn't allowed to come home until the work was finished and by that time it was already dark. If my mother took one day off, she could get in big trouble and would have been punished by being denied food, and if she took three days off, she could have been executed. At approximately 8:00 P.M. when my mother returned home she called her daughter's name and found her dead body lying on the ground. Three months later when I was allowed to visit home for a few hours, I noticed my baby sister was missing. When I asked where she was, my mother told me with a very mournful voice and tears that she was dead. I was shocked and cried out "It can't be her, you are lying to me!" I felt very sad because when I was sent to work outside the village, she was running around and playing on the ground. I used to carry her and kiss her, she was so beautiful and healthy, why did it have to be her? I cried very hard and didn't want to go back to work, but I had no choice. If I had refused I would have been executed. I thought it was just a nightmare. I waited for three more months and when I came home again, she still was missing. Then I knew it wasn't a nightmare after all. It was true. I still refused to believe that it was her life that God took away from my family, but that is what happened. For four years I tried to forget all about her, but every time I thought of her I felt very hurt and sad. I can't help it, I still think of her even today and will for the rest of my life. Anyway, we lived under those horrible circumstances along with others for four years.

After the Vietnamese Communists invaded our country early in 1979, we were allowed to go back to live in the city. I was then ten years old. My parents decided to go back to Phnom Penh, but when we got there, we found the place we used to live was empty and destroyed. My parents decided to go back to the forest and to escape, but we had no destination. We followed somebody else's footsteps. If we were in luck, we would survive, and if we got caught, we would all die. We had to escape as soon as possible, for if we stayed there any longer, we were going to die of starvation and illness. Finally, we gave it a try. Those people who were trying to escape, including our family, could only travel at night when the Vietnamese soldiers were sleeping. It took my family and the others approximately three days and four nights to escape to the border of Thailand. There we had to walk through deep mud, dead bodies, jungle, and fallen trees.

During the middle of our escape, something happened that forced my family to stop our flight. During the whole journey, my three-month-old baby brother hadn't cried at all. But when we got almost to the Thai border, he started crying very loudly. He just wouldn't stop. We knew that if we continued walking and running, the Vietnamese soldiers would hear the baby's crying. We were traveling with ten other families, about eighty people including my family, and other people didn't want to get killed. So they said to my parents, "If you want to follow us, you have to kill the baby." My parents were confused. They didn't know what to do because it was in the middle of the forest. Finally, my parents made their decision. They were not going to continue with the group any longer. They would rather save the baby. My parents said, "If we are lucky, we will survive, and if we are unlucky, then we will all die." So we let all the other families continue on their way and we waited until the baby calmed down. Luckily, there were three families who wanted to stay and keep us company. We didn't want them to get killed, so we tried to convince them to leave with the other families, but they wouldn't listen to us. They said that my family had helped them a lot in Cambodia and they couldn't just leave us alone. In order to repay us, they would rather risk their lives accompanying us. We were very proud to hear that, we all agreed, and we thanked them for staying with us. For twelve hours, the baby wouldn't stop crying. We weren't thinking of giving him up yet, but on the other hand we and the other families were very shaken. If the Vietnamese soldiers caught us, there go our lives, heaven or hell, we wouldn't know.

After a long while resting under a big tree, one of the families found a small cage which seemed more or less like a bird's cage. Inside of that cage there was some old food which had been there for quite a while. That "cage" was a spirit house, so we all went to look. We put some water and rice in the spirit house and prayed to the ancestor spirit to help the baby stop crying, and help us all stay away from danger. It was amazing! It was a miracle! A few hours later, the baby stopped crying and then we continued our escape. In the middle of the road, there were hundreds and hundreds of people dying. Some died by stepping on the mines that were buried by the Vietnamese soldiers, sometimes right by the border of Thailand. There were thousands of skeletons crossing one another, facing in all directions. Some of them died with their eyes closed and others died with their eyes opened. Some of them died with mouths opened trying to yell for help. When we finally caught up with the other people, we heard that the six families who tried to convince my parents to kill the baby had all died by stepping on the mines. Luckily, we didn't follow their directions and kill the baby. The three families who had stayed with us all survived. When we left to make our final push to the border, there were no soldiers, no mines, and no trouble. Our final move to the border of Thailand was "a piece of cake."

After we got to the border, we were sent to stay in a refugee camp called Khao I Dang. In comparison to the previous years in Cambodia, the Khao I Dang camp was a pretty neat place to stay because there were food and clothes provided by the United Nations. In addition to this, there was a school for children and elders. We also had some freedom. We lived there for eight months and one week. We made our living by selling Cambodian pastries and meats.

One day the Cambodian translator announced on the microphone that if people wanted to go to another country, they should sign up for it. We signed up to go to Texas, because my father's brother, his best friend since childhood, lived there. Several months later a letter came back that said that our family was too big to fit in one house. The government refused to let my father's friend, whom we call "Uncle," sponsor us. At the same time, we also sent some photos and names to another uncle, my mother's brother-in-law, who lives in Brookline, Massachusetts, but he couldn't sponsor us because he had lived there for just a short period of time. In the meantime, my uncle from Boston sent us some money and helped our family until he could find a sponsor for us. He took our names and photos and showed them to a few churches. It was really difficult for one family to sponsor a big family like us. Finally, at the end of 1979, we were accepted by the United States of America sponsored by the United Methodist Church.

We were really happy after we heard that we were to have a chance to go to America. To us, we see America as "freedom and heaven." We couldn't eat or sleep because of happiness. Before we could come to America, we had to first pass physical exams. We passed all the exams and three days later we were heading for America. We traveled by plane for eighteen hours from Thailand to San Francisco with one stop in Japan. After we arrived at the airport I felt very strange, first of all because I hadn't had a chance to adjust to the cold weather in this country. Second, I felt very strange in my ears because of the language I couldn't understand. We stopped in Los Angeles and lived in a hotel for forty days until the church sponsors found us a home in Lynn, Massachusetts. We lived with our sponsor in Lynn for one year and three months until we found ourselves a home. We were well taken care of by the people who sponsored us but we felt as if they wanted to own us because they fought each other over us.

There were not just the deaths and the horrors that we had faced in Cambodia during the Communist regime; there were obstacles such as language, American attitudes and behavior, and climate, that we also had to adjust to in the United States. For instance, regarding language, since we were the first Cambodian family living in Lynn, it was very hard for the American sponsors and my family to communicate about things we needed like rice, chopsticks, soy sauce, and certain kinds of food. We had to use the Khmer-English dictionary to translate all the words.

For three and a half months we experienced the American attitudes and behaviors. When I first came to the United States in late 1980, I was shocked to see that American people varied greatly. Their white skin looked so smooth compared to our color of skin and their sizes were big compared to our body size.

Since I and other Cambodians did not know how to speak a word of English at first, most of the American people did not want to talk to us because they thought that we were nothing like them. When I walked to school (I knew how to speak a few words of English at that time) I would say "Hi" or I would give a grin to every American student I encountered, but they paid no attention to me at all. They pretended that they didn't hear me. Another time in English class, I didn't understand what the teacher was trying to say so I asked classmates sitting next to me to explain it, but they pretended they were busy. They felt that their friends might laugh at them if they answered me. They acted like that because I was different, I came from another country, spoke broken English and looked different.

When I first heard that my family had been selected to come to the United States, I was very excited. I felt like I was going to heaven since I expected that life in America is full of freedom and nice friendly people, so different from Cambodia. I also thought that I would be very happy and would make a lot of American friends. Instead, people insulted me because of the way I looked and talked.

Another example of the differences we experienced: I saw teenagers standing in the street holding hands and kissing in public. I was really surprised because in Cambodia holding hands and kissing is uncommon. Even if people do hold hands and kiss, they do it in private, but, really, you hardly ever see young people holding hands and kissing.

Finally, the last difficult obstacle was the climate, especially during the winter. It was weird and strange to see white dirt on the ground. And the weather was so cold; we had never felt so cold before. We used to live in a climate that was warm all the time. For the first few months, we all had colds because we didn't know how to dress warmly enough, although now we are accustomed to it.

At school I was like a person from another planet. I was totally confused, my ears hurt. I got a headache almost every other day because I couldn't understand what other people were saying. It drove me crazy! After three months, we were put in school. I was then eleven years old, but I was placed in the same classroom with my two other brothers. That classroom combined all Southeast Asians from first to sixth grade. I was placed in sixth grade, but because I knew very little English, I still had to learn to write my name, color pictures, and do other things. After I knew how to write my name and how to greet people, my teacher told me that there was no need for me to stay in that class any longer.

One year later, I was placed in junior high school as a seventh grader. I took my courses in an ESL program (that is English as a Second Language). The first quarter I didn't make the honor roll, but the other three quarters I did. I was moved up to eighth grade a year later and made the honor roll and super honor roll. The principal took me out of the ESL program and placed me in regular American classes during the second quarter. I didn't make the honor roll in my third quarter because I got one C in math, but during my fourth quarter, I made it again. After eighth grade I went to high school for four years and then came to the University of Massachusetts, Amherst, continuing my education in the field of human services to learn how to deal with people, especially with Asian people. I speak two Chinese dialects, Mandarin and *chao jiu*, Khmer, and English. People are needed in human services because many Asian people have a hard time understanding English. Cambodians are still coming to the United States. I hope that I can help these people with their problems. This is a challenge and opportunity for me. If I ever succeed, I'll know who I am. Right now I am just a student with a few experiences. Someday I hope that I'll be a successful career woman. I'm going to make everyone in my family very proud of me.

A couple of years ago, I never thought about my own country after it had become Communist. Everything was broken into little pieces and many hundreds of thousands of people died. I just said to myself, "Forget all about it. It's not worth it. It's the past. Let's just forget all about it." Suddenly I realized that that is not right. I was born there and I should remember it. I was very young then, I knew very little about my culture. Studying at the university I have learned many things about my parents' beliefs and attitudes. I think that some of my classes have helped me in dealing with my Southeast Asian heritage. For some time I didn't even know who I was, whether I was an American or whether I was a Cambodian. Now I know so much about my cultural background that my family is very proud of me.

VIBORA LIM

Migrating to America

My father, Bit Seang Lim, being well informed of the war conditions in Phnom Penh, brought our family to the Cambodia-Thailand border in April 1975. After a two-week stay at the border, our family defected to Thailand. The downfall of Cambodia to the Pol Pot regime forced my family to leave our native country to search for freedom elsewhere. This critical period was the begining of the adaptation process that our family experienced. Furthermore, there has been an enormous cultural transformation in language, traditional values, and social status. These and other changes that have taken place in our lives will be presented in detail in this paper. First, I will briefly discuss my family's background.

My father, Bit Seang Lim, was a commander in Cambodia. Born into a wealthy Cambodian family, my father was sent to France to be educated. After completing an accounting program at a university, he returned to Cambodia. Upon his return, the Cambodian government offered him the opportunity to train to become an officer in the army. Without hesitation, he accepted the chance. Not long after, he married my mother, Kina Bun, who is Chinese. She is the daughter of the owner of a local bakery shop in Phnom Penh. The marriage was arranged by their parents.

My parents have three children. Vichhana is the oldest child and the only daughter; I am the middle child and the oldest son; and Vimatey is our younger brother. In Cambodia my parents enrolled me and my sister in private schools. We attended different schools.

Vichhana attended a French-Cambodian elementary school, while I attended an American-Cambodian school. Since the Americans were involved with our political system at that time, my mother thought it was best to enroll us in different schools. She thought that our family would be better off if we had this sort of language flexibility.

As far as I can remember, everyone in my family was happy back home. To this day, my mother frequently reminds us how "well-off" we were. She stresses that not only were we well-off economically but that we also had high status and power in our community. I don't doubt my mother's claim; I think I was too young to realize and appreciate the things we had.

In late 1974, conditions in Phnom Penh were getting worse day by day. I recall that everywhere I went, something reminded me that our country was at war, like the uniformed soldiers with American M-16 rifles guarding our villa, army jeeps parked in our driveway, and tanks roaming the streets. At the banquets held at our house celebrating my father's promotion to a higher rank, the main topics of conversation among the guests were usually war related. Once in a while, I would hear stories about the fighting that went on outside the city. The stories made me feel sorry for the soldiers who were involved in the fighting, but I never felt threatened when hearing them. I perceived the war as fighting that occurred far away from the city of Phnom Penh.

The sound of bombing was not uncommon at night. In fact, in late 1974, the bombing became so intense that my father forced everyone to sleep in the living room where the walls were reinforced. Not long after that, my father brought our family to an army base which was located near the Thai border. My sister and I were told that we were on vacation in Thailand. Everyone back home assumed that we were vacationing.

Near the Thai border, we stayed in a small town called Tmar Pouk for two weeks. There was another family that traveled with us, the Ming family, who was the family of my father's colleague.

On the evening of April 15, 1975, we left Tmar Pouk and headed for Thailand. We traveled in three American army jeeps. The jeeps were driven by local soldiers who knew the back roads well. I remember the rough ride through the dark roads. We must have driven for eight to ten hours before we reached the border. It was sunrise when we reached Thailand.

After a two and a half hour drive in Thailand, we were

approached by the Thai police. The Thai police handcuffed all the men traveling in our group and then took us to their city jail. There we were all locked up in two separate cells; females in one cell, and males in the other. I was put in the same cell as my father. This was the first time that I actually came in contact with the Thai people, so my initial impression was that they were evil and rude. I cried and cried until one of the guards opened our cell and took me to my mother.

Within twenty-four hours the Thai official informed us that the Communist party had taken over Cambodia. The Thai officials kept us in the cells for two weeks before one of the Thai officers took our family into custody and took us to his home. I was surprised and confused to receive the warm hospitality of the young officer and his family. I asked my mother why they were being so nice to us, and she told me that there are good and evil types in every people.

From what I understood, our case was pending because the local officials did not know exactly what to do with us. In the meantime, my father was desperately trying to contact his associates in Bangkok. My father did not have much luck; everyone he tried to contact was not available or never returned his calls. All the people who my father once knew simply turned their backs on him. We stayed at the officer's home for six weeks before the Thai officials transferred us to Bangkok, where higher governmental officials would handle our case.

The prison in Bangkok where we were kept was larger and more contemporary than the last one we stayed in. To my surprise, there were quite a few Cambodian people there. This time I was not separated from my mother, only from my father. By this time our family was separated from the Ming family and the other soldiers who defected with us. In the Bangkok prison, my father ran into an old friend of his, Mr. Luong. Mr. Luong also defected from Cambodia, but because he had connections with the American embassy in Bangkok, he was able to make arrangement to leave for America. Mr. Luong was kind enough to contact the embassy for us, and he explained to the Americans our family's situation. Within two weeks, all the official documents were completed, and our family left for a U.S. Army base in Thailand, where we awaited our journey to America.

We stayed at the army base for a month before departing for America. It was early September 1975 when we made our journey. I recall that morning clearly. Everyone in my family woke up early to get things organized. I was very excited, especially after hearing all the fascinating stories about America, but I kept the feeling to myself because my parents were sad. My mother cried during most of the trip, and there were signs of worry, confusion, and uncertainty on my father's face.

After twenty-three hours of flying, we finally reached our destination, the Los Angeles airport. The moment we got off the airplane, we all received winter jackets. Many things fascinated me when we first arrived. When walking through the entrance gate, the first thing that caught my attention was a color television set. Then I saw people drinking Coca Cola from a can. Never before had I seen such things. Everything was so clean, and everyone was well dressed. All the fascinating American stories were a reality to me.

The U.S. officials brought all the Cambodian refugees to a military base south of Los Angeles. Everyone remained in this base until the resettlement agency found sponsors for the families. The waiting for sponsorship was long. The twelve-week stay there was responsible for our family's making many adjustments. The greatest adjustments we had to make were in our eating habits. American foods such as hamburgers, hot dogs, or macaroni and cheese did not satisfy our appetite for spicy foods. Everyone in my family adjusted well to the food, except my mother, who was so depressed that she hardly ate.

Schools were set up in tents to teach the older people English, American culture and customs, and other basic survival skills. Church organizations frequently came to donate clothes and toys. Some Cambodians considered converting to Christianity after seeing how kind the church people were.

The agency finally found a sponsor for us, and we were scheduled to relocate near our sponsor's home in December 1975. Our sponsor was Mrs. Anne C. Mrs. C. was an older woman, probably in her early fifties. She was an entrepreneur; she owned a business that arranged banquets for all special occasions. Mrs. C. was divorced and lived alone with her son. The first thing she did when we arrived was to take us to our half-furnished apartment in Los Angeles. Next we went shopping for food at the local supermarket. I have never seen such a place, where almost all the foods were packaged. Since we did not know what most of those packaged goods contained, we only bought what we could identify, basically rice, meat, and vegetables.

For the next couple of days, Mrs. C. spent time with us, helping us get familiar with the things we needed to know in order to survive. She brought us to the local welfare office and helped us apply for aid. We learned how to use public transportation and became familiar with the neighborhood. I was enrolled in the fourth grade, and my sister was enrolled in the fifth grade at an elementary school nearby. Through Mrs. C., my father obtained an office job in downtown Los Angeles doing clerical work. My mother, who was having the most difficulty learning English, stayed home and took care of my brother.

Attending school for the first time in America was difficult for me. I did not know what was going on in class, what I was supposed to do, or what was expected from me. My first teacher in America, Mr. Yoon, was Chinese. I was impressed by his ability to speak English like any other American. Every time he asked me questions about schoolwork, my only response was to nod my head. Everyone in class would laugh when it was my turn to answer questions. I hated school. Soon I started playing with American kids during recess and after school. I made a lot of friends at school. This interaction with Americans helped me develop my English-speaking ability.

Mrs. C. was very kind to us at the beginning, but after our family settled down, she was a totally different person. She started to take advantage of our family. She asked us to help out busing tables at her catering business every weekend. In return we received leftover food from the banquets. Occasionally, Mrs. C. even asked my mother to sew for her. My mother did not like the idea of providing personal services to Mrs. C., especially when she was not getting paid for it, but she did it because she felt obligated to Mrs. C. for helping us settle down.

My father was not happy with his part-time job. He knew he was capable of doing technical work and that the only thing holding him back was the language barrier. He enrolled in a nearby community college and took English-speaking and -writing courses. He excelled in those courses and was quickly able to speak English reasonably well. My father continued with his education by enrolling in UCLA. There, he worked on his masters in education. Not long after his enrollment in UCLA, it was time to renew the lease for our apartment. Mrs. C. refused to renew it for us. Since my father only worked part time, he did not have the credentials necessary to meet the lease agreement. My father explained to the manager of the apartment that we had enough money to pay for the rent. He told the manager that our source of income was from his part-time job and government assistance, but the manager still refused to renew the lease for us.

Being frustrated and upset with Mrs. C., my father took us to Boston. He also wanted to move to Boston because Boston had a reputation for having some of the best educational institutions in America. I was really excited about moving to Boston because I had never seen snow before.

We moved to Boston in early 1976. My father was able to find a one-bedroom apartment. At this period our family ties fell apart. My father wanted to go to school, but at the same time he had to support his family. He took a job as a dishwasher in a Chinese restaurant at night, and attended school during the day. Every little thing started to irritate him. He and my mother fought often. Those arguments usually resulted in my father physically abusing my mother. I hated it when they fought. I wanted to help my mother, but I was too small to do anything. The abuse continued until one day my mother threatened my father, saying that if he touched her, she would call the police. I recall her exact words, "If you touch me, I'll call the police, this is not Cambodia, this is America. You can't beat your wife and get away with it. I'll have you arrested if you touch me!" From that day on, my father never laid a hand on my mother.

My father left our family two months after we arrived in Boston. He never told us where he was going; he just came home one night from work, got his things, and left. We were isolated in the sense that we knew no one. We were not familiar with the city and we did not speak much English. There was a Chinese family that lived down the street from us. My mother, who speaks many different Chinese dialects, went to the family for help. The family took her to a Chinese help center in Chinatown. She explained her situation to them. Without hesitation, the Chinese community provided us with help. They helped us with food and shelter until they found a job for my mother. My mother worked at a sewing factory in Chinatown. With the income she received from her new job and help from the government, we were able to survive. As time progressed, she was able to move on to find better jobs. Eventually, we were no longer dependent on government assistance.

Many changes have taken place since the day we left Cambodia. For one thing, there has been a drastic change in the language spoken in our household. My little brother and I have the hardest time maintaining our native language because we interact with English-speaking people more than anyone else in the family. When we first arrived in America, I knew how to read, write, speak, and think in

Owning a car is one step on the ladder of entry into American life.
Photo by Sam Pettengill.

Khmer. Now I speak Khmer at home, and the only thing that I can write in Khmer is my first name. My sister has been successful in maintaining the Khmer language. Because she is older and speaks Khmer with her husband at home she has constantly maintained her native language. This language discrepancy creates communication problems within our family. It has been difficult for us to express our ideas, concerns, and feeling toward one another. We often misinterpret each other, which results in conflicts.

In addition to adopting the new language, our family also adopted the new culture and way of life. We celebrate holidays such as Christmas, Thanksgiving, and Halloween, all of which we did not celebrate in Cambodia. The new culture sometimes conflicts with the old. For example, my mother did not approve of my sister getting married because the marriage was not arranged. Also I recall an incident where I had to make the choice between being Americanized like my peers or holding on to old traditional values. This was when I had to decide between going on a date or complying with my mother's wishes and not going. Sometimes it is difficult to be faced with two different values and sets of customs.

Today, the whole family is fully adjusted to life in America. My mother is no longer the wife of a military commander, but she is an excellent saleswoman for a jewelry store. She has become a very independent and proud single parent. I admire my mother for being so strong and for not giving up hope during hard times. Through observing the Cambodian families who settled in America later, we realize how lucky we were, and we have learned not to take anything for granted.

MAX HARTSHORNE

From the Killing Fields to Greenfield: The Story of Chard Houn

CHARD HOUN, a Cambodian refugee, has been in the United States since 1983. Like so many others from his country, Chard suffered through a lifetime's worth of struggling and brutality during the eight years he endured the mass insanity that made up life under Cambodia's Khmer Rouge government. He can talk matter of factly about mines going off and about watching people being forced to walk off cliffs into pits, and at first it doesn't seem real. Maybe he has made the whole thing up. But the grim details are too bizarre to come out of anyone's mouth as fiction, and you realize that this slightly built twenty-year-old really did live through what many have called the world's third holocaust.

His story is mostly bits and pieces. The quotes are his own words, the phrasing and word choice have not been corrected, and the greatest emphasis was placed on getting his words across in the context of what we have learned in class about life in Southeast Asia, particularly Cambodia.

Chard Houn was born in Sisopom, a city in the Battambang province of Cambodia, in 1965. His parents owned a restaurant and an import business, and they lived above it. Chard recalls that the family worked a lot, and that there were always people around when he was growing up. He remembers that his father liked politics and soccer, and that he too was interested in politics, though he was discouraged early from getting involved.

> "My father told me once that we had to go with the Communists. He said they were just people like us. . . . I was so interested in it, he said 'Why do you want to know about politics?' My mother and sisters never paid any attention to it, my father always said 'why do you want to know that?' "

Chard Houn's room is on the third floor of a Greenfield rooming house. There is no window, only a skylight which lets in pale, dusty light. On the wall there are posters of Sylvester Stallone, posing as Rambo holding a tremendous gun and, next to him, Clint Eastwood. We spoke on several evenings about his long road from "the killing fields" to Greenfield. One of the first things I asked him about was Rambo, though he did not explain his reasons for idolizing this star who has made millions by acting out the murdering of Southeast Asian people. Chard just likes these two actors and Bruce Lee, and doesn't see the connection that is so ironic to me, his American interviewer.

We began by my asking a question that Dith Pran addressed during his talk at the University of Massachusetts. Why did Cambodia's nightmare happen?

> "The Khmer Rouge have psychological problems, they just kill so many people, no reason. I wish you could tell me how people can do things like they do. At night, husband sleep different place than wife, 'cause they don't want them to hear them complain against them. They walk around your house and see if they can hear you complain; they come in and kill you if you complain."

How did you survive? Why didn't you get killed?

> "Well, you know, just lucky, I was lucky. Whenever the full moon was out, they'd make the people work all night . . . with just a little bit of food."

Were you able to make friends with people during those times? It must have been very scary, and you weren't that old.

> "People sometimes is hard to talk to each other, because they are so scared. The children work for the Khmer

> Rouge they teach them when they are seven or eight, 'when you hear them talk about something, just tell us'; the children kill their mothers and parents. They turned the children against their own parents.
>
> "This country is a hard situation. I have bad dreams every night. Boom, boom, I wished they had killed me. I can't stand to see the people killing you know, sometimes the kids would just unload their guns on people, or put a knife up to my throat here like this. Some serious suffering I saw . . . people having dinner and a bomb drops and legs go flying here, heads, go there."
>
> What things do you miss about Cambodia the most?
>
> "First of all my parents, my brothers and my sisters. And our place."
>
> What do you think it's like in Cambodia right now?
>
> "Probably Soviet, or Vietnam, boom, boom, boom. To live like that, under the Communists, it's hard, you have to rebuild everything. You know they destroy everything, machinery, factory, they exploded it and wrecked it. That is so stupid . . . that's why they just killed all the professional people. One of my friend's father was killed while he was taking a shower, just boom, right in the water."

For Chard, the beginning of his road out of Cambodia began with one too many acts of senseless killing. Even as a young teenager of fourteen, he knew that he had to get out and at that point he decided to leave for good, and he did what so many millions of his countrymen had done before him. He headed west. The trip took three weeks.

> "I lived in the jungle by myself, and tied myself up in the tree in the jungle, and once this pig came up to me and started licking my feet. I didn't know what it was. It was a friendly pig, he was scared away from the farmers, this pig was a friend, he lived with me in the jungle. After the

Khmer Rouge killed him they tied him up the tree, and I see the smoke, and I couldn't find him, and I see him hanging, and they are eating him. I was so angry, I ran up and took the M-16, and threw it into the stream, and I just walked away. I almost shot Khmer Rouge, but there was too many people. Then I decided I was going. I just walked toward where the sun set, west. Three weeks. No food, all there was was fruit on the trees. There were three groups, Vietnamese, Khmer Rouge, and Sihanouk. I met up with a guy who lived in my village, but he got scared and ran back. I didn't run back. Soldiers catch me, after I hide for three days under a tree, where animals live. They bring me to refugee camps, and I start my life there in Thailand.

"When I see the movies, the violent movies, it seems to me like a joke, people said, 'Did you see that violent movie' and I say, 'Naaah.'

"I was eleven years old, and I did it, slept in trees like a bird, tied myself up there, you know. There's a lot of people who did it, you have to find a way to survive. I had to survive. When I live in the city, I didn't have family, how did I get food? I know sometime I gonna die anyway. I have friend, I meet some people. This country, you know, kids eighteen, know nothing about that, when I was nine years old, I knew, it's very very hard to see your parents, boom, think about friends, boom, house, boom, sisters, brothers, boom, it's very hard. The Khmer Rouge were brave and mean young kids. It's very hard to tell you all this stuff, 'cause when I talk, I see. When I do anything, I can see everything . . . you never believe this, that's OK."

What would you like to do here in the United States?

"If I could, I would like to get into politics."

What's your memory of Prince Sihanouk?

"He was always the king . . . people in my country always respect him. On TV and on the radio, I heard him, and saw his picture in the papers. But King Sihanouk lied and was a very dishonest man. Sihanouk, he is a bad thing too, you read that people have learned about the torture, the human rights, about justice . . . if they learn this, then they will learn about Sihanouk, both China and Sihanouk, they just come and take all the money from the government and gamble, they are bad people.

"People don't pay any attention to the politics . . . that's why our country collapsed. Because they believe in the Buddhist idea that they should not kill anybody, that's why when the Khmer Rouge come they destroy religion, they destroy temple, smash everything. People killed. You know who Pol Pot is, you know, in fact he is much like Qaddafi. He tried to change every move he made, hard to figure out, he's crazy. The Khmer Rouge, they said they had to clean our city, that's when they said we had to leave. They came with megaphones, and drove around and said everyone had to leave, they say, 'Now, leave now.' It was bloody, and they were shouting; it was night, everyone was crying; we had to walk thirty miles to another town, where nobody lived, where we had to build a new house. About three or four months later, they picked me up to take care of cows, and I was separated from my parents.

"My country respect Americans very high . . . my people like Americans, they always are helping, when people are sick, they make them comfortable. But when Pol Pot and the Khmer Rouge come, they teach people to hate Americans. That made it very hard. They have a song, make Americans go back, but those people (Khmer Rouge) are stupid people, from the jungle.

"I became a good worker, because I was afraid of dying, so I just work harder and harder, in the gardens where they grew food for all those people. After Vietnam took over Cambodia in 1979, people were free to go out and try to find their families, but I couldn't find them. I did find my old village. I could not find my old house in the city, it was boom, boom, just destroyed. But I couldn't find my family, my brother. I was living in the refugee camps for three years. There is not enough food there. It is very boring. They have school there, we play soccer, but it is boring. I know a lot of people, Americans who worked at the refugee camps, and I knew a lady who was from Boston, while I was sick in the hospital, she helped to find me a place to live in America with a foster family."

What was the most shocking thing about this country which struck you when you first arrived here?

"The buildings, all of these kinds of cars, I hadn't seen that for three years . . . it seemed like everything full of happiness, you know, when I saw this place.

"When I first came here, I lived with my foster parents in Granby, but I didn't get along that well. It was boring, I had to stay home all the time, just go to school, and come home, study, go to bed. Granby was a lot of surprises . . . all these buildings, cold, and snow, I hadn't seen before. There were three kids in the family beside the parents. The most difficult thing to adjust to was how they talked, and so many times my parents were so quiet, they didn't talk, just come home from work and not say anything. I couldn't understand anything, I was so confused, I didn't know what's going on. I tried to commit suicide, it was hard to handle. Things were not right, my English was not good, I was so confused. Then I moved to Whately, and went to Frontier High School. I wanted to be independent, so I finally moved to Greenfield; I decided to go to GCC and take English as Second Language classes and other classes. Now I can decide what I want to be.

"I think this country is newer than Cambodia, one of the hardest things to get used to is the scenery, not being where you grew up, not having your relatives. My country is kind of more friendly than this, the way they react to you here is different, my country is more close than here. Sometimes, like here, if you want to go over someplace, you have to call first, in my country, you want to see your friends, you just walk in.

> "My country, drinking is not a major problem, it's just nothing. The kids smoke pot so much here, I can't believe it. In my country, that marijuana grows in the ground, it grows like grass, nobody touches it, they use it for cooking sometimes, not very often. I was surprised to see how people smoke it here. I couldn't believe it was illegal here, nobody does anything with that plant in Cambodia. I don't believe that kids go out and have some pot and get drunk. Kids here, too, I don't believe how they go out and have sex; in my country you have to have parents' permission, get married first. That surprised me, too. I am pretty mad sometimes you know, the kids, the youngest are to respect the older, the schools teach, no matter what you are, the older get respected. Here I can't believe the kids, they the boss, they look down to the older people. We look up to them. So much different here, the kids bang on the tables, and shout at the teacher."

Chard Houn's experiences in America so far are mixed ones, tempered by the reality of what he has lost, and the knowledge that he must adapt to a different culture forever, since there does not seem to be any choice back in Cambodia. He talks about wanting to get into politics and lacks the inherent apathy that makes up a good deal of the American population of twenty-year-olds.

Like millions of other Asian immigrants who have come to America during the 1980s, Chard will no doubt adapt to and help to change this country. With him comes a world of understanding of things too horrible for most of us to even imagine. Rambo would certainly benefit from listening to the wisdom of his fan.

From Laos

NILANDONE PATHAMMAVONG

Left Empty and Longing

My name is Nilandone Pathammavong. People here call me Kai. "Kai" means "Chicken." I am the oldest of eight children. I have one brother and six sisters. They are all in school at the present time. My family and I are now living in Springfield, Massachusetts. We came to this country in 1978. We left Laos, my native country, in 1976, a year after the Pathet Lao, Communists, had taken over Vientiane, the capital of Laos. The following story is based on my life after Laos became a Communist country; later I'll return back to the life I had before Laos became a Communist country.

Based on my memory, it was not until 1975 that the Pathet Lao completely controlled Laos. Before that time they had small provinces under their control and in 1975 they achieved control over Vientiane.

I remember that in 1975 there was a parade along the main street in Vientiane. People were showing how happy they were to have the Pathet Lao control the country. People held signs that said "Long Live the Pathet Lao." I was only eleven then and I didn't know what was going on. I asked my parents and was told that Laos was becoming a Communist country. I didn't know the meaning of the word "communism," so I asked my parents again and was told that the word "communism" means everyone will be treated equally. Everyone has equal rights. There won't be the "masters" and "slaves." No one will be a boss. You will decide for yourself what to do. Even though I was young, I still didn't believe that Laos would be a better place to live than before.

Because I could see from my parents' eyes that they were crying, I could sense that they were hiding something from me.

During the first month after the arrival of the Pathet Lao, there was nothing else but the news about welcoming them on the radio stations. Along with the news, there was also a program in which interpretations of contemporary events were presented by MoLum (trabadour singing, a type of lyric oral musicians whose origins trace back to the twelfth and thirteenth centuries). People who were on the non-Communist side called these performances "The brain-washing musics." The purpose of this music was to change people's ideas about communism. It was to make them believe that Laos would become a very peaceful and just country in which to live if everyone were willing to cooperate with the Pathet Lao.

A month later, things didn't turn out as the Pathet Lao had promised. The school system was changed. Instead of having French and other foreign languages, they only had Russian in the high school. Every student had to perform an extra hour of group work in the school garden or somewhere else in the town. Students hardly had any time to help their parents. Most of the time they had to spend with their group and do the work together. Students were told that by doing work together they would have more work done in a shorter period of time. The more they worked, the better the country would become. I remember, I saw my teenage cousins working very hard. For some of them, working hard was the most terrible thing that had happened to them in their lives. They felt they never had worked so hard. I remember, I worked in a group just once because I was in the elementary school. They didn't expect much work from us. Only students from the junior high, high school, and the institution had to work hard.

Besides the changes in the school system, there was also a change in the army camp. There was an announcement that said that any army officers who were willing to volunteer to go to the reeducation camp in the northern part of the country to learn more about the new system in the communist society would stay there for a shorter period than those who were forced to go. For this reason, most of the army officers signed up for the trip to the reeducation camp. They were promised that they would be returned to Vientiane in six months. Three of my uncles signed up for that trip.

Unfortunately, things didn't turn out as promised. Those officers are still in that reeducation camp. This camp was called "the camp for brainwashing." They are being treated as criminals. From what I've heard, some were killed or buried alive. There were some who were lucky enough to escape to Thailand. In the last few months, my cousin sent us a telegram from Laos saying that one of my uncles who had been in that camp since 1975 had died. The Communists said he died because he was very sick from starvation and there was no medicine for his sickness. Some thought that it might not be starvation that caused his death. His wife who had gone up to visit him said he was all right, he looked pretty healthy to her. What really happened was that the Communists had put him to sleep by giving him a poisonous shot. He was a colonel in the Royal Lao Army and they wanted to get rid of him. If that was so, I am very happy for him. I couldn't bear seeing him working very hard at his age. He had never worked that hard in his life. Right now, there are two uncles of mine in the reeducation camp. I hope to see them come back home safely. I hope nothing bad will happen to them. I can picture them working in the hot rice field just as it is shown in the film *The Killing Fields*. I don't want to make it sound as if I were selfish, but thank God my father was not one of those army officers. My father was a captain in the army. He too had signed up for the class; luckily he was still needed to work in his office. My father is a very bright man. He speaks four different languages fluently: Lao, Thai, English, and French. In the office where he worked, there was no one else who could speak both fluent French and English. Therefore, he was still kept by this ministry.

But this did not last long. After a man who worked with my father (a Communist) learned how to run the office, my father was no longer needed. One day, a secret letter arrived at my father's office. The letter stated that my father would be ordered to go to the camp in Phongsaly in northern Laos. Luckily, my father was told this before he received the order. He then made plans to leave Laos. He asked the doctor to write him an official letter saying that he needed a rest for a week. (He had a nervous illness.) My father then took a week off. During that week, I remember seeing the worried look on his face. He didn't tell my mother about his problem. On the last day of his vacation, he found a way to escape to Thailand. He left home that night and did not take much with him. (It's impossible to bring a lot of things with you while swimming across the river anyway.) He took some money, his clothes, and the family picture with him. I remember that the night my father left, after he had gone, my mother came to my room and woke me up. She asked me to go inside her room and then told me that my father had already gone to Thailand. At that moment, it was the first time in my whole life that I'd even felt I was losing someone I really loved. My mother and I both prayed for the safety of my father. We both cried all night.

My mother said that before he left, he came into our room and took a last look at each of his children. Tears streamed down from his eyes. He did not notice that with every step he made, my mother was keeping her eyes on him. She knew he was going to leave her and us, but she was afraid that if she cried or yelled she'd give the Communist army a signal and they'd come to arrest my father. That's why she kept silence all night until my father had really gone. She said she even followed him to the river where he and his friends escaped together. (My father's friends were two of my cousins who had also tried to escape from Laos, and my uncle who went back to Laos to get my father after he got the message. My uncle was already in Thailand, but he went back to Laos to do his business and then later came over to our house to help my father escape.)

The next morning my mother put all of us in the car, hoping to follow my father to Thailand that day. But there were so many of us, and my youngest sister was only nine months old. The man who was supposed to take us across the river was scared. He said he was afraid my sisters would be frightened and cry and make a lot of noise, which would give the Communist guards or the patrol boat a signal that there were people trying to escape and they would shoot us. He suggested we go to another town far from the city where there were fewer soldiers and where it would be less dangerous. My mother then took us back home. We lived there for a whole month with painful memories.

Life was very difficult without my father, especially at supper time. Without my father the dining table seemed so empty, even though there were still eight of us there. None of us could mention my father to anyone, not even to relatives. Since the day my father left, my mother had been seeking a way to take us to Thailand. A week later, my mother received a letter from my father. He said he was all right. He asked my mother to go and see his aunt who lived in the countryside away from Vientiane, to discuss with her how to escape from Laos. My father said she would be able to help us even though there were so many small children in our family. (We were told that there were only six Communist guards in her town and that they were friends of my aunt.

All she had to do was ask them over and cook them some food in order to keep them away from their duties during the night we would escape.)

Two to three weeks later, my mother took us to my aunt's house. At first she didn't tell us where we were really going. She said we were going to visit my uncle in another part of the city. I knew she was lying. If we were going to visit my uncle, why then did my mother take a long look at anything that would remind her of her people. She had to take all those personal items including the family pictures, my father's certificates, his secret notes and files, and also some valuables that were given to her by her mother. I didn't ask her any questions. If I did she'd probably feel very bad or maybe start to cry. (She did cry, because her eyes were red.) I helped her pack some of my brother's and sisters' clothing. I was told not to take too much, just enough for six or seven days.

It took almost all day to get to my aunt's house. She lived with her husband and some other people who were there to help her with her store and also her rice fields. (She gave them money and food and in return they helped her with her rice fields.) We stayed with them for two days. The second day, we were brought down to my aunt's hut which was about ten kilometers away from her town. The hut was surrounded by nothing but rice fields and was very isolated from the rest of the town. We stayed there overnight.

Early in the morning, about 4 or 5 A.M., we began our escape. No one was allowed to make any noise. All my sisters and my brother seemed to understand what was going on. They sat quietly in the small pirogue. As we left the riverbank, my cousin and an old man paddled the pirogue quietly. I saw the tears flowing down my mother's face. Then I started to cry too. I took a last look at Laos. I could sense that I wouldn't see Laos again for a long time. My thoughts were back in my hometown, wondering what my cousins were doing at that time and how they would react when they found out that we had gone to Thailand. I missed all my relatives very much, especially my grandmother. (She died three years later, in 1979.) I cried even more when I thought about not seeing them again. It took us almost two hours to get to the other side of the Mekong. (Longer than a usual trip to Thailand.) It took that long because it was raining at the time and also the pirogue could not be paddled fast. We had to be very quiet and be careful not to make any noise so as to not alarm the Thai patrol.

Two hours later, we arrived at a very small town in Thailand, Ban Phone Pheng. My cousin took us to her friend's house. She introduced us to her friend. After she talked with them, she and the old man went back to Laos. We stayed at my cousin's friend's house for three days. The house was built in the ancient style. It seemed very strange to me. I couldn't sleep the first night. My mind was wondering what was going to happen to us before we would see our father again. I tried to close my eyes and force myself to sleep. I stayed awake the whole night. I got up very early the next morning. The old lady cooked us some food. I couldn't eat because everything surrounding me was so strange. I didn't know those people who I was sharing the meal with. (They were very nice people, but they were still strangers to me.)

My mother asked me to eat a little, so that the old woman would not be upset. (Because she would probably think that I didn't like her food, or that she was not a good cook.)

The second night we all went to bed early. (We had to get up early in the morning to get ready for the long trip to see my father.) I was very excited about seeing my father. (I guess everyone was, especially my mother.) The next day, my mother gave an old man some money to rent a car. He drove us to the camp in Nongkai where my father was. It took us all day to get to the camp. Along the way, we made many stops at police stations. The police checked every passing car for illegal immigrants. We were the illegal immigrants at the time. I didn't know what the old man told the police, but we didn't get caught.

We arrived at the camp that evening, around six o'clock. My mother gave a man some money to take a message to my father. Half an hour later my uncle came. He said my father was having an interview with one of the American consul about coming to the United States. My uncle took us back to where he and my father lived. (They lived in a barrack made from bamboo. There were sixty or seventy barracks in that camp.) Once we got there, we waited for our father to come back. Forty-five minutes later, he came. He and my mother hugged each other for a long time, they both cried with joy. Then my father gave each of us a hug. We all cried. At that moment I felt like I was dreaming. I never thought I would see my father again. I thought I had lost him forever.

My family and I lived in the camp for exactly a year and ten months. Our lives in there were terrible. Life would have been worse if it were not for my father's teaching. He taught English to those who wanted to go (or were going) either to the United States or to Canada. He used the money he earned to buy food and to buy us some clothes, and the rest was saved to build a school for my father, since he had been teaching in individuals' rooms.

There were eighteen people including my family who lived in two small barrack rooms. (The other nine were my father's stepbrother and my mother's nephews and nieces.) The rooms were just big enough to sleep in. All my sisters and I shared the same bed. My brother shared with my stepuncle. My parents slept in the bed next to mine in the one room. My uncle, my brother, and the rest slept in another room. My uncle built a porch as a place to eat, next to our rooms.

There were approximately fifty families living in each barrack. Each family had one room regardless of how many people there were. Food was provided three times per week, except for the rice. Rice was provided once per month. Each person received the same amount of food. This given food wasn't enough for our family, nor for any of the others. Only a limited amount of meat, fish, vegetables, and rice was provided. We had to provide for the rest of our needs.

My family and I were supposed to leave for the United States a month after we arrived at the camp, but because my father wanted his stepbrother and my cousins to leave at the same time, we were told by the American consul to wait for another year. (We found out later that it was a waste of time to wait for another year. Because there were so many of us, the American consul was afraid my father wouldn't be able to take care of us all, especially in a big country like America where everything depends on the head of the family.) From then on, all I ever dreamed of was coming to the United States. I heard my father say that life there was much easier than life in our country, Laos. There was a good future for everyone in a big country like America. (There was no future for us in the camp. Tomorrow would be just the same as today.)

My father also said that life would be much easier in the United States if we knew some English. He suggested that I and my sisters and brother take a class with him, but because my sisters and brother were too young to learn at the level our father taught, and because they hadn't learned French before, my father sent them to another school. They started from the beginning to learn to speak English. I learned English with my father for a year and a half. My father taught during the day and also at night.

Life was not easy in the camp. There was much violence going on: stealing, fighting, arguing, and killing. People were frightened into confessing, and they didn't know what to do with their lives, so they got uptight and did stupid things. Some might think that stealing is the only answer for money problems. (To me, I think only the lazy ones and stupid ones didn't know how to solve the money problem or any other problems. Some people went out and worked on the farm for money.)

Most of the thieves or problem causers were found to be in the teenage groups, people whose parents were still in Laos or who had no parents left alive. Looking back at this situation, I consider myself very lucky. I left Laos with my parents, and stayed with them in the camp. I had enough food to eat and enough clothes to wear, and even a place to learn English. I didn't have to worry about where my next meal was coming from. All I worried about was my future life. I wanted to leave the camp as soon as possible.

On May 28, 1978, my dream finally came true. We received a letter from the American embassy saying that we would be leaving for the United States in one week. We were all happy. I kept picturing myself living in a new country and a new home, and speaking a different language.

The next day, my mother went out shopping. She bought goods that might not be very common in this country, for example, sculpture made from wood, a rice steamer, and all kinds of herbs and spices. She also bought us some new clothes and new shoes.

Two days before our trip to Bangkok, my parents invited the monks to come over to our place. We had a ceremony called "Soukhovan." Our relatives and friends came over to wish us "Good Luck" in the future. After the ceremony was over, we ate together. (My mother and her friends had prepared a lot of food for that day.)

For us, "Soukhovan" is the traditional way to say goodbye and wish luck before traveling. We tied a string around each other's wrist. This string was believed to contain our spirit, our soul, and was also believed to give a safe trip and protect us from being afraid of height. (Some people fainted if they were far from the ground.)

The following day, I remember my parents took us to the harbor. From there we could see Laos on the other side of the Mekong River. Once we got there, my father tried to look for a good spot where we could see clearly. A moment later he said "Well children, I want you all to take a good look at Laos because this will probably be your last time seeing it." My two youngest sisters probably didn't know what was going on. They were too young to remember Laos. I wonder if they knew where we were going and where we were at that time. (Poor sisters!).

Later on my parents took us to a Chinese restaurant, then to a movie. After that we went back to the camp to get ready for the trip to Bangkok.

We arrived in Bangkok at night. The trip took all day. (It's a very long distance from Nongkhai to Bangkok.) We stayed in a temporary camp for nine days. Everything is very expensive in Bangkok due to the size of the city and also because of the life-style. Bangkok is a very big city and very civilized compared to Laos.

The day we were waiting for had finally come. It was June 14, 1978. We were taken down to the airport. We waited for an hour before getting on the plane. It took exactly two days to come to the United States from Southeast Asia. We first stopped at Kennedy Airport in New York. An hour later, we were on another plane. Our final stop was at Bradley International Airport, Hartford, Connecticut. At the airport, my grandparents, my uncle and his wife, and my aunt were there waiting to pick us up. After we took all our baggage, we were brought down to my grandparents' house. We stayed there overnight.

The next day we moved into a house that my grandfather had already rented for us before we arrived in this country. This house was in Manchester, Connecticut. (It's about fifteen minutes from Hartford.)

A week later, my father took us to school and signed each of us in. I was put in eighth grade. My younger sisters and brother were in seventh, fourth, third, kindergarten, and the Headstart program. A couple of weeks later, my father bought a used car, a station wagon, with the money that was given us to start a new life in this country.

School was tough in the beginning. I understood what people tried to say to me, but I had a very hard time responding to them. Because I had already learned some English, however, things didn't turn out so bad as they did for others who didn't know English before they came to this country.

It took me a couple of months to improve my speaking. From my experience, I learned that the best way to learn new words was to read a lot of books and use the dictionary to find what the words meant. None of us seemed to have any problem in school. I found out that young children could learn the language much faster than adults. This was because they were adapting to another language that might not seem like a different one. To them, it was just like learning their own language. This was because they didn't go to school before, and English was the first language they were learning.

Three years later, we moved to Springfield. My father got a job as a counselor at Job Corps. We bought a house there, and we moved into our new house on June 18, 1981. I didn't like living in Springfield until I went to school, made new friends, and got acquainted with my neighbors. Then I began to like Springfield. I graduated in 1983 and got accepted to the University of Massachusetts. I am studying industrial engineering.

Before the Communists came into Laos, our lives were much different from how they are now. In Laos, we had our own house. We didn't have to pay any utility bills such as phone bills, electricity bills, water bills, and heat bills. My father received one big (100 kg) bag of rice every month. This was because he was an army officer. Our family was considered middle class. We had a house, a car, a television, a telephone, a refrigerator, and others things that many families did not have. Therefore I always considered myself one of the very lucky children in Laos. My parents put me in the best school in town. It was a Catholic school, a private school run by nuns.

The school system was a little different from here. For example, instead of receiving letter grades such as A, B, C, D, E, we received different places in Laos. The student with the highest point in class would be placed in the first place, the next would be placed in the second place, and so on.

During elementary school, I was one of the best students in school. For every class, I was placed in the first place. My parents spent extra money to put me into the summer school to learn more French. They told me that one day they would send me to France to learn to be a doctor. That's why they wanted me to know more French and why they put me in the best school in town. They planned to send me to Paris right after my junior year in Laos.

Obviously, things didn't turn out as planned. The Communists took over Laos before I even got a chance to go to the junior high school. I thought my whole future would end at that time. I thought I'd never become a doctor. There went my dream.

But I was wrong. Here I am in a very big and civilized

country and becoming an engineer. What else could I ask for? I am satisfied with the way I am. My parents are here, and so are my sisters and my brother. All that matters is that we are all happy here in this country. Even though I am very happy with my life now, one day I hope to return to Laos and live there once again.

CHANTHAVA CHANTHAVONG

One Last Long Look at My Country

My name is Chanthava Chanthavong. I was born in Savannakhet, Laos. I lived in a medium-sized house which was roofed with sheet metal, had stilts, brown wooden walls, six windows, and a vast porch. The house was surrounded by mango trees, papaya trees, and palm trees which made the house cooler in the summer. When I turned six, I started at Chomkoe, an elementary school, where I went for three years. I enjoyed attending that school because I made many friends and I learned many different things about my country.

My father operated a machine for hulling rice, fixed water irrigation systems, repaired Japanese cars, and loved to work on farms. Once a month my father would appear at the door with a paycheck for my mother to support our family. My mother stayed home to take care of us four children. She accepted full responsibility for her children by making sure that they had enough to eat. No matter what happened in the neighborhood we lived in, my family always stayed together through the good times and the bad times. However, the happiness did not last very long because the Communists took over Laos in 1975.

On a quiet evening in 1975 at five o'clock, the Communists came to our town. The local people were ecstatic in their welcome. These troops wore dirty green uniforms and caps. They looked very pale and exhausted. I saw some people throwing flowers and leis toward the Communists to show them how much respect Lao people had for them. Within an hour the whole city was in turmoil.

Chanthava Chanthavong and a high school friend.
Photo by Sam Pettengill.

The prime minister of Laos was Souvanah Phouma. He allowed his Communist brother, Souphanuvong, to take over the country. Souphanuvong promised his brother that when he took over there would be peace and prosperity in Laos.

The Communists took away the Americans, the aristocrats, and those who worked for the Americans. Since people in Laos disliked the tortures, bombs, killings, solitary confinements, and the confiscation of properties, they secretly attempted to escape.

My father who worked for the Americans in an agricultural development corporation was found out by the Communists in 1978. They found his identification card and noted it was written in two languages. The next morning the Communists were going to send my father to a solitary confinement camp on a mountain, in the northern part of Laos. My father came home with a frightened expression. It was about nine o'clock; I could hear my parents discussing the document, but I did not quite comprehend the whole story. My mother was so scared about my father that early the next morning she went to the governor to get permission to visit her village. The governor returned the document to my mother. As the time got closer and closer to eight o'clock the weather turned foggy and it began to pour. My mother had formed her plan to escape. She paid two men to rescue my family. Of course, at that time I believed my mother was going to visit her village. When the ferry boat passed my mother's village, I realized something was wrong. I asked, "Mom, where are we going?" She replied, "This is the last time you will see Laos." Tears started to run down my face. Suddenly, two men fired rifles and pulled my brothers, sister, and me into one canoe. Meanwhile, my parents were in the other canoe. I could hear my baby brother screaming and crying because of all the chaos. The two men paddled the canoe as fast as they could so that the Communists could not see us. It took approximately two minutes to cross the river to Thailand. I held my little brother in my arms with tears running down my face and trembling because I was petrified by the firing guns. I sat on a log near the shore looking back at my country, but there was no hope.

Abruptly, the police came and dragged my father away and jailed him in Nakhon Phanom, Thailand. I did not even get a chance to say good-bye to my dear father. My mother met a Thai woman who took us to her home and allowed my mother to work in her rice field. As the months went by, my mother saved up enough money to bail my father out of prison. When my father came home he built a bamboo house which consisted of thatch, bamboo, small logs, and wooden stilts. My mother kept me at home to take care of my brother. While in that house I received a letter from my uncle who lived in the United States. He wrote us a letter to convince us to come to America. He explained in the letter that my family should register at the Ubon camp.

When my family moved to the Ubon camp, I encountered many things. Everybody at Ubon camp had to have an identification card with special numbers. Food was provided for the refugees, but everyone got a very small amount. I can remember the time when my mother sent me to wait for food. There were many people in line. I was standing with my wooden bowl watching the people around me. I could hear some people yelling at each other and babies crying. The line was extremely long. I was getting exhausted and aggravated. My forehead began to perspire. It was my turn to get some food. The old man gave me half a fish which stank and a head of chinese cabbage. I wanted to cry because I did not think it would be enough for my family. I scurried home and began to think, "Why do I have to suffer so much!" All of a sudden my tears started to fall. Fortunately, my mother was an expert cook. She made the tuna into soup within thirty minutes. My whole family enjoyed it tremendously. After a wonderful lunch, everyone sat around the house. I usually sat beneath a papaya tree singing and talking to myself. Sometimes I would stare at a handsome boy who happened to walk by. This particular afternoon was unusual. I sat next to the mail box waiting for a letter from the United States. While I was waiting, the mailman dropped a letter into the box. He said, "You are a lucky girl." I did not know what he was talking about. I opened the letter and it was written in English and Laotian. I read it and rejoiced because I was going to America.

Early the next morning all the people who were listed to go to America woke up early. We left Ubon camp by bus at six o'clock. I was on a plane at eight o'clock. I had never been on a plane before; therefore, I was scared to sit on the seat cushion. I sat on the arm rest. The stewardess told me to sit properly. I was sitting for almost twelve hours. The plane landed in Hong Kong because they had to get some fuel. Outside it was completely dark. One of the officials took my family into a hotel room. In order to get to the hotel, we had to go on an escalator, which frightened me to death. I refused to step on it because my first impression was that it might cut off my legs. A guard at the escalator carried me up to the hotel room. I screamed and struggled to get away, but he was too strong. I was thirteen years old.

The next morning the plane left Hong Kong early for Tokyo. From the plane I saw buildings and the terminal, which reminded me of my country. The building was square and built of cement. It had bars on the windows. I saw the mountains that surrounded the airport. The plane arrived in Alaska. I saw snow everywhere. I asked, "Mom are we in heaven?" She did not know that white stuff on earth was snow. My family was transferred to a different plane. The refugees were being separated from one another because people had to go to their own sponsors. My sponsor was my uncle and the World Church Service. The stewardess took my family to board a plane to Washington, D.C.

We finally arrived in Rockville, Maryland. Unfortunately, things did not turn out the way I expected. I slept all day and at night I was awake because of the change in time and the different environment. For approximately three months I did not attend school. Every time I walked out the door the American children started staring at me. I guess they probably thought I was some sort of strange creature from another planet. Then I started to school in Rockville. I was illiterate in English at that time. The school required foreign students to attend "English as a Second Language" class. I studied real hard because I wanted to be literate in English. After a year my English rapidly improved.

It was a cold evening and I was sitting in my bedroom trying to study my English book. I heard a phone ring and I picked it up. On the other end was my mother's relative who wanted us to come to Greenfield. She felt isolated from the people in Greenfield. My mother had pity for her and she decided to go to Greenfield.

In addition to describing my life and my journey to Greenfield, I also want to mention that I have an ambition. Someday I hope to go to school for four years to get a bachelor's degree in arts or science. I do not expect to become a doctor or lawyer. I want to help people. It does not matter what kind of job it is as long as there is a chance to help people. Just because I am going to college does not mean that I want to be rich. The truth about me is that I lack education. I do not understand the world and the people around me. I am not a smart person, but I know that I will try my best to accomplish my goal.

Finally, I am satisfied with my life and my past. God has

created me this way. There is nothing I could change. I think I am a very brave person who has struggled through many hardships. If someone had been in my shoes he or she probably would say that she or he had a terrible life. For me, as long as I have faith in God, a pillow, blanket, shelter, and food, it is a good life.

Chanthava was a high school senior attending a university class when this essay was written.

CHANTHA SOUVANNA

New Hope for a Disheartened Refugee

NIGHT passed. The new day had just arrived. The light spectrum began to clear away the darkness and undefined views in front of my eyes. Then the sun began to shine all over the sky. The jungle, lifeless at night, came back to life again. One more time, animals began to search for food. The birds were flying from one tree to another. Some of them sang in their own languages and voices, but some of them just flew around and enjoyed the morning sun. The humans also began to prepare themselves for their individual chores as they tried to make a living.

As the sky got clearer, I was still lying in bed. It was about 6 A.M. and I wondered, "What day is it?" I suddenly realized, "Oh yes . . . today is Friday, March. . . ." I stopped to think awhile, "March, yes . . . I've got it. Today is Friday, March 16, 1979." I said to myself, "Oh no! I still have one more school day." I didn't know what to do. I kept my eyes closed and relaxed in bed. I got out of my bed as I heard my mother calling me to prepare for school. Oh well! another day, another dollar? I forced myself to get up and prepare for school as usual.

Even though it was a long time ago, I can't forget that little road on the way to school, with spring flowers on the other side. It was like a road at Disneyland. The flowers looked fantastic and they smelled as beautiful as perfume. My friends and I often called it "a little sweet expressway." It took approximately twenty-five minutes for me to get to school. However, on that Friday, when I got close to school, I suddenly changed my direction. Instead of going to school, I went to the shopping mall which was located right in downtown Vientiane and very close to my school. I was just walking around and looking for something to do.

After three hours in the mall, I felt exhausted. When I walked out, I looked up into the sky. I saw the sun had risen up into its highest altitude. Its heat was felt all over the place. It was hot. I could see the sun's heat on the road. I was soaked in sweat. At the same time, my stomach started growling for food. It was frustrating, so I bought some candy bars and headed to the beach on the Mekong only fifteen minutes from the mall.

It was probably noon when I spotted the beach. I hoped to see some beautiful women lying and taking a sunbath there. But too bad, there were no Laotian women who seemed to like the beach. This is different from America.

I then started walking across miles of open field filled with sand on the Don Chan beach, alone. The temperature was still hot and humid. I was totally exhausted. My legs were as tired as my hands and body. I could hardly walk. But thank God for my health, I finally made it. As I got closer to the water, I felt very strange. I heard a sound like somebody whispering in my ear and telling me to do something that I never thought of before. I wasn't sure what my mind was thinking of at that moment.

I thought about many things: one of them was the danger of escaping. Suppose the Communist soldiers saw someone trying to escape, what would they do? Of course, they would kill. Everybody knows that. Large numbers of people were killed while attempting to escape. When I thought about this I was nervous. But I was very lucky. As I looked around, there wasn't anyone there but me. I then bravely made a decision to escape.

I took off my shirt and left it on the shore with my shoes. I then quickly went into the nice cool but fast water and started to swim. When I made it through half way, the water started to form waves. It looked very scary. It was not a joke. It was a real and dangerous risk I had taken. After a while, I found myself getting closer and closer to the Thai shore. God! I was very happy, but "Ooop, what is that?" I said to myself. "If I don't die today, I feel like I'll live forever." I saw the water in front of me spinning hard in a circle and forming a giant hole that was capable of pulling anything going by to the bottom of the river. My heart was pumping faster and faster, probably one hundred beats a minute. Worse,

Worse, the water had pulled me into that giant hole. Somehow I struggled out of it. Wait! This time I almost gave up, I let the water push me to wherever it wanted to because I had no energy left. All of a sudden I felt that I had gained a very special energy. "I have come this far," I said. "I must not give up now, no matter what!" I then strongly swam against the current and I finally landed in Thailand for the first time in my life.

When I had just landed on the Thai shore, I looked back to the opposite side. My emotions then started to build up. Here I was alone in a strange land. I couldn't speak their language too well, but I could understand some of the words they said. Also I didn't know where I was. In addition, I was hungry and cold. "Where should I go from here?" I looked back toward Laos one more time, before I went to register as a refugee at the police station not far from the shore.

Right after my registration, I was sent to prison for two weeks. In there, I could hardly breathe because it was too small and crowded. The atmosphere was terrible. At night, I was cold and had no place to sleep. I couldn't move my body. I sat in front of the toilet door all night long. Every night I always looked at the clock and wanted it to move faster so I could get out and stretch.

Two weeks passed. I was transferred to a concentration camp for another two and a half months, then I was released to the Lao refugee camp, Nong Khai, in Thailand.

My life in the camp wasn't too bad. I spent a year and a half there, before I came to the United States. During the time in the camp, I spent about a year living with neighbors and the rest with my family until I left the camp.

Living in the United States and living in Laos is different. For example, living in Laos is like living in your own fantasy. Most Laotian people have their own property such as houses, rice fields, and many have land. The most important is their own freedom. The slow-moving society of Laos doesn't disturb its people at all. Everybody is supported. People who worked in the city didn't have to worry about living conditions, because the pay they earned each month was enough to cover the food cost, mainly rice. On the other hand, people who don't have a job would go out farming, perhaps hunting, to make a living. Everybody was happy just the way they were.

In the United States it is very difficult to make a living. First of all, the language is the main problem for all newcomers. Second, the living situation is also a problem, because of the experience of adjusting to the jobs. And third, most people are trying to adapt to the new society. In addition, when people are trying to fit in a new society or a new culture they always adopt the new culture and religious beliefs, especially young people.

It is hard to compare the differences between the two cultures—living conditions and other things. However, I had to struggle for a while when I was younger. Now I am very happy to be living in the United States and to have an opportunity to pursue my dreams, especially education.

LAMTHIANE INTHIRATH

A Change of Cultures

In Laos I find it quite usual to come from a family with eight members. A feeling of pride and honor comes to my mind when I think about my family. Only through hard work and cooperation have we come to know success as a large family. We have always lived together as one big happy family.

My mother is a Thai woman. She came from a wealthy noble family from Chaingmai. My mother went to Ramkamhang, one of the most popular universities in Bangkok. She graduated with a B.S. degree in business administration in 1960. She went to Laos two years later and she opened a business there. She was married to my father in 1963, and had my sister a year later, but my sister died at birth.

My father is half Chinese and half Lao. His father is Chinese and his mother is Lao. However, my father was born in Thailand and grew up in Laos. Way back in Laos my father was in the Lao FBI, working for the former Laotian government.

We came directly to Ubol, Thailand, in 1975. My family was lucky in not having to be locked up in a refugee camp like other Laotians. We were not special or anything like that, except that we had some money. Almost anything is possible for people in Thailand if they have money. For example, my family was not supposed to live outside the camp but we did. My father had made an arrangement with the camp's mayor. My father, mother, brother, and I were allowed to live in Ubol, Thailand, like other Thai citizens because we were born there. However, other people in my family, including my other two sisters, my

Preparing rice by steaming in a basket
(village, north Laos).
Photo by Joel M. Halpern.

grandmother, and my aunt were not allowed to live there because they were not Thai citizens.

My father wanted to stay in Thailand because we were attached to it and we thought it would be good for us. Unfortunately it did not work out the way we wanted because the citizenship registrar asked for too much money from my father to make false citizenship papers.

In 1979, my father sat down and carefully took the time to plan a trip across to this country. He told us that the trip would be a permanent and memorable one. I came directly to Leominster, Massachusetts, in September 29, 1979. I did not know any English when I first came here. I was very frightened for myself and my family. Moving into a different country and environment is not easy for anybody.

Living in the United States was not easy for my family then. We had many difficulties and problems as newcomers. Communication was the major problem for us. We did not know how to communicate with our sponsors and neighbors. I could not even tell them that I was sick from the airplane. I was afraid I would not fit into American society. I was afraid I would not assimilate and would not adjust. Food was a second problem for my family. We had never eaten American food before and we did not know how to eat it. My grandmother who was sixty at that time especially had difficulties; she refused to touch anything for quite some time. I realized it was difficult for her to adapt because she was too old for it. It was a culture shock for her and for all the people in my family. I do not expect any sixty-year-old person to learn how to speak English, to like the cold weather, or to like the food in America. My sponsors did their best to help us; they went as far as to take us to McDonald's. I did not like hamburgers then, but I do now. I have become assimilated, readjusted, and adapted to a new culture.

During my second week in the United States my sponsor took me to school; I registered. The official said I could start school in a few days. He was pleased to have me as the first Southeast Asian student in school. That particular morning I got up early. I put on my newest clothes, which my sponsors had bought for me. I was full of excitement to meet more people, but deep down inside I felt afraid of something. I spent a little time with other students. I felt uneasy and frustrated when I could not speak English. When other students met me they would ask what my name was and where I came from. I could not respond and then they laughed at me. Often I took it the wrong way and got upset with them. I was not an unfriendly person. I wanted so much to express myself and tell them who I was. I think almost every newcomer experiences the communication gap.

I was very frustrated when I could not speak English so I was motivated to learn English faster than others. I was able to communicate with other students within a few months. It was because of my learning ability that I was awarded thirty-five dollars during a Thanksgiving Day rally. I also received a perfect attendance certificate in the eighth grade. The local newspaper interviewed me as the first Southeast Asian student and an outstanding student.

I remember one bad experience I had during my freshman year in high school, my second year in America. I could speak a little English then. I was sitting in the study hall quietly and trying to keep my mind on my books. Some boys were bugging me as they had been doing for the past few weeks. I tried to ignore them, but they still bothered me. They called me a "Chink" because they thought I was Chinese. They laughed at me when they saw me and threw cookies at me. I realized that I was different, but I did not expect other students to treat me like that. My frustration built up and I came to the point that I had to do something about it. I had to stand up for myself; if I did not, nobody would. I knew the consequences, however, I preferred to end the ridiculing right then than have them carry it on. I got up rapidly without giving the boys a chance to move from their seats. I threw my math book in one of the boy's face. I woke up the whole classroom. The teacher asked what I was doing. I told him exactly what had happened. I thought he was going to send me to the office for detention, but he did not. Instead, he sent those boys down and they got two days after-school detention. After two detentions they realized I had the same feelings as others, they made an apology and it was accepted. Shortly we became friends.

I graduated with honors from Leominster High School in 1984. During my high school years I participated in the girls' soccer and swimming teams. In my senior year I was a homeroom representative and a yearbook member.

My favorite hobbies are meeting new people, studying, working, and going to the beach. I love going to the beach, and I love to have my picture taken. Beside those interests I also take my work

Lao food continues to be enjoyed in New England, prepared and served in a traditional way.
Photo by Sam Pettengill.

seriously. I would like very much to become successful in the future, not only for my own benefit but also to prove that a Laotian refugee can have a professional occupation just like other people can. I realize it is a long tough road for me, but I am willing to work hard and to give up some years for more schooling.

NGUYEN HUNG ANH

A Poem: Tet Ly Huong—Away from Home at Tet

Translated from the Vietnamese by
Lucy Nguyen-Hong-Nhiem

Xuân này đã mấy Tết ly hương?
Đại học giao kết bạn bốn phương.
Sớm hôm mài miệt pho kinh sách,
Đêm ngày vật lộn câu khảo hạch.
Tết đến tạm thời dẹp bút nghiên,
Quây quần tưởng niệm đấng tổ tiên.
Nâng chén trà dư, không bánh mứt,
Ôn chuyện ngày xưa, khuya chẳng dứt.
Người cha bỏ mạng chết thảm sầu
Trong tù tập thể tận rừng sâu.
Mẹ nghèo gầy guộc, tay run rẩy,
Lam lũ tháng ngày trên nương rẫy,
Miếng cơm manh áo những thất thường.
Đời sao bể khổ ngập đau thương?

Xuân này đã mấy Tết ly hương?
Tết đến gần xa khắp phố phường.
Nhớ thuở ấu thơ trên đất mẹ,
Đón xuân nhộn nhịp nô nức thế!
Bây giờ cách xa xuân vẫn đến,
Nhưng đến làm chi, thêm mủi lòng?
Chẳng biết mẹ hiền cùng thân quyến,
Đàn em thơ dại, có vui không?
Bạn bè mấy đứa ở xa đâu?
Kẻ ở tù, người kinh tế mới.
Người yêu nay đã theo bộ đội.
Đời sao bể khổ ngập thương đau?

How many times have I spent my New Year away from home?
I made friends from everywhere at UMass/Amherst,
They came here to devour books and books,
Day and night to struggle with exams.
At Tet let us temporarily put our pen aside,
Let us gather together and remember our ancestors,
To sip a cup of tea without cookies and candies,
To recount old stories until late night.
Father gave up his life sorrowfully,
In a concentration camp in the deep woods;
Thin mother, with shaky hands,
Toils days and months at furrow in a field,
She eats and clothes herself sparingly.
Why does life become a sea overflowing with misery?

How many times have I spent my New Year away from home?
Tet arrived here and there on every street corner.
I remember my childhood in my motherland,
When I welcomed Tet with excitement.
Now, although away from home, Tet comes anyhow,
But why does it come to bring only sorrow?
I wonder if my mother and relatives
And younger brothers and sisters are happy?
Those few friends I see no more,
Some in prison, others at the New Economic Zone,
My sweetheart already married to a Communist comrade.
Why does life become a sea overflowing with misery?

ERVIN STAUB

Commentary: Human Destructiveness and the Refugee Experience

I was in the midst of writing *The Roots of Evil: The Psychological and Cultural Origins of Genocide* and had already finished an analysis of the "autogenocide" in Cambodia, when I was invited to attend a meeting of the ongoing seminar on Southeast Asia in which the student essays were generated. I heard one student describe in personal terms the horrors in Cambodia that I knew so well from my research. But the tragedy of students from other Southeast Asian countries was also manifest in this meeting: young people, children and adolescents, fearing for their lives or in the hope of greater security and human dignity left their countries, alone or with their families.

Being a refugee is a tragically common human experience. Unfortunately, repression and violence that lead people to escape from their own country and seek refuge elsewhere have always existed. It is all too frequent in our century. Huge numbers of people were displaced and became stateless in Europe during the first part of the century. Millions of people became refugees in the wake of the Second World War. But this saga seems never ending, and the flow of those seeking refuge continues. This book tells part of the story of young people who came to the United States as refugees from Southeast Asia.

For over two decades now, I have been studying the roots of caring, of altruism, of people helping others, as well as the roots of violence inflicted by groups on members of other groups, the roots of extreme human destructiveness. My own experience—surviving the

Holocaust as a Jewish child in Budapest, living in a Communist country afterward, escaping from Hungary after the revolution of 1956 was defeated by overwhelming force, and coming to the United States in 1959—had to provide some of the seeds of my concern as a psychologist (and a human being) with altruism and aggression.

Over four hundred thousand Hungarian Jews (out of a population of a little over half million) were killed by the German and Hungarian Nazis, and a total of five to six million Jews were killed in Europe. While many were willing to kill, and most people removed themselves from it all, I and most of my immediate family survived because some people cared. I owe my life to the Swede Wallenberg, who totally committed himself to saving the lives of Hungarian Jews as they were being transported by the Nazis to Auschwitz. I experienced the caring and willingness for self-sacrifice of a Christian woman who worked for my family and who endangered her life to help us in various ways. She smuggled food, for example, into the house in which we were tenuously "protected" by documents created by Wallenberg as a representative of Sweden and, following his example, by the embassies of a couple of other countries. She brought food not only for us, but also for the many people crowded into this large apartment house.

What are the roots of the human destructiveness that creates refugees? How are refugees affected by having to leave everything behind, and, in many cases, of having undergone great suffering, pain, or danger before they leave? What are the obligations of bystanders (if any), of individuals, and of nations?

CREATING REFUGEES: THE ORIGINS OF REPRESSION, TORTURE, MASS KILLINGS

The experience of refugees greatly varies, as the accounts in this book show. I will briefly describe and discuss what happened in Cambodia, as an example of the most extreme human destructiveness. Some of the same societal and psychological processes are involved in lesser destructiveness as well.

A group of young Cambodian students in Paris, all members of the French Communist party, comrades in Communist study groups, became political associates and, ultimately, associates in designing a vision of a society that they attempted to fulfill by genocide. Their road from Paris in the 1950s to winning a civil war in 1975 and gaining power both over their enemies in the civil war and among the Cambodian Communists was a long one.

Once they came to power they killed many officers in the army and government officials, many professionals and intellectuals—doctors, teachers, lawyers. These people were enemies and judged incapable of building and living in the society that Pol Pot, the prime minister, and his associates designed—a society based on the land, on the peasantry, totally self-sufficient, with complete equality among members.

They evacuated the cities and drove people into the countryside, forcing them to build villages from scratch, without expertise and without help. They made these people spend long, long days building irrigation systems or working the fields. Although there was an extreme shortage of food, they prohibited the gathering of food from the forests, a traditional mode of survival at times of scarcity in Cambodia. They established many stringent rules of conduct and killed people for even slight infractions, at times after one or two warnings, at times without warning. Practices varied somewhat in different areas of the country and during different periods of the four-year rule of the Khmer Rouge, as the Cambodian Communists called themselves. With less than total consistency, they broke up families. Through direct murder and starvation they killed perhaps two million people. They imposed profound suffering on all.

How could human beings treat other human beings as Pol Pot's Khmer Rouge treated the people of Cambodia? A very basic human tendency is to differentiate us from them, the ingroup from the outgroup. While the potential for this is part of every person and every group, persons and groups can greatly differ in us-them differentiation, and even more in the devaluation of "them," as a function, respectively, of their personalities and of their culture and social organization.

To a lesser or greater extent, members of outgroups are usually devalued. In extreme instances, they come to be regarded as less than human. As a result they are excluded from the "range of applicability" of moral values. The usual principles of morality and of respect for human life and human welfare are not applied to them.

At times, due to a combination of difficult conditions of life in a society and of certain characteristics of a culture, an ideology evolves or an existing ideology is adopted that offers the vision of a better life, a better society, a better world. The ideology offers hope, a renewed comprehension of reality in place of the chaos and disorganization that at such times usually rule society, and a sense of significance in working to create a better world. Normally, in order for the ideology to be adopted it has to fit the culture, it has to embody elements of culture or of historical experience. Commonly, such "better-world" ideologies identify one or more groups of people as enemies, as people who by their basic nature and very existence, or who by their characteristics and modes of conduct, interfere with the fulfillment of the ideology. At times the majority of a society may be regarded as an obstacle to the better world.

As members of a movement commit themselves to such an ideology and strive to gain power, they often develop a fanaticism. The ideology becomes a goal that must be fulfilled at any cost, a goal overriding all other goals. Any and all means become acceptable to fulfill the ideology. The welfare of human beings, of individuals or devalued groups, becomes unimportant. People become objects and are treated as such. To create this better world some are tortured and killed, others are "reeducated," and a majority of society may be kept in a state of repression, deprived of basic rights.

Ideological systems are likely to create the most refugees. Much of this discussion also applies, however, to repressive systems in which the prime reason for the repression is to maintain privilege and power. Over time, people come to see their power and privilege as their right, as justified. Those with power and privilege sharply differentiate between themselves and other groups. They devalue the less privileged. Another common human tendency also enters, "just-world thinking," seeing those less privileged, those who suffer, as somehow having deserved their suffering. Paradoxically, this happens even as people themselves inflict suffering on others. Finally, there are often ideological justifications for maintaining a system of privilege and repression.

THE EXPERIENCE AND PSYCHOLOGY OF REFUGEES

The impact on refugees varies depending on the nature of the repressive system in a country and the individual experience of the victims. There are commonalities, however, in any experience of repression, threat, and danger, in escape, and in entry into a new society.

Human beings have certain basic needs. They need a

feeling of security, a freedom from danger and threat of attack. They need some feeling of control over their immediate fate and their future lives. They need to believe that they can protect themselves and fulfill their essential goals. Important for both security and a feeling of control is at least a moderate trust in the world. People also need a sense of connection to other people, some feeling of community. Under the conditions that lead people to escape from their homes and start life in a different country usually none of these needs are fulfilled.

The conditions that create refugees may lead to the experience of total helplessness in face of the brutal power of the system. Depending on the extent that they are singled out as a limited subgroup of society, members of victimized groups may develop a growing self-doubt and self-devaluation: Am I persecuted because something is wrong with me? This happened to many Jews who were persecuted by the Nazis and others; it happened to Armenians as they were persecuted (and about a million of them killed) in Turkey; it happens to mistreated minorities in many countries. It happened to Cambodians, especially city people and the educated who were driven from their homes. And those who were not killed were degraded, mistreated, enslaved, forced to witness others' degradation and murder. Their experience must lead many refugees to a view of the world as hostile, dangerous, unpredictable.

The experience of refugees will profoundly affect both their worldview and their self-concept. Their feelings of helplessness may be counteracted as refugees initiate their escape and entry into a new country. After all, in highly significant ways, they are taking charge, they are exercising control over their lives. This may strengthen their belief in their capacity to create a new life for themselves. In addition, as people move to a new country, the sharp break makes it possible for them to discriminate between the old and the new, to be aware of the greater benevolence of their new environment, of freedom and possibilities.

Still, at deep levels, basic effects remain. Those who experienced extreme cruelty and great suffering may be left with deep wounds: doubts about their self-worth, about the goodness and trustworthiness of human beings. In most refugees, a feeling of vulnerability and a sensitivity to danger may be easily reawakened. Former refugees describe their anxiety upon encountering policemen, agents of repression in their former lives, or upon crossing borders, which reminds them of past insecurity and homelessness. Hostility directed at them may have greater impact, may threaten them at deeper levels. I have experienced these and other revivals of a dormant but still existing self.

THE ROLE AND OBLIGATIONS OF BYSTANDERS

What is the obligation of other human beings toward refugees and toward the destructiveness that creates refugees? A basic obligation of those who offer refuge is true acceptance and hospitality. Refugees, human beings much like ourselves, have experienced pain, suffering, and the collapse of their former existence, and they have a deep need to create a new existence. We must reach out to refugees as we hope others would reach out to us. As a nation we must open our doors to those who are persecuted and in danger, whether from El Salvador or Cuba, regardless of the political ideology of the system that they are escaping from. All nations have practical limitations, in resources and space, but within those limitations, which are less restrictive for a large and wealthy country like the United States, we must open our doors to innocent victims.

But there is also another profound obligation. You and I and our nation as a bystander must not ignore the suffering that countries around the world inflict on their own citizens. We must not deny that it is happening, or close our eyes to it and ignore it, as the United States and Britain and many other countries did during the Holocaust and at other times. As the genocide in Cambodia began, the world was very slow to respond. Moreover, all too often ideology or "national interest" shapes the response to perpetrators and inhibits help for victims. When partly in response to self-destructive provocations Vietnam invaded Cambodia and put an end to the murderous Khmer Rouge rule, our government and China joined as strange bedfellows in recognizing the ousted Pol Pot regime as the legitimate representative of Cambodia in the United Nations.

Individuals, groups, nations of the world, and the community of nations have an obligation to exert the maximum influence in their power, which is great in the case of the United States, to stop governments from mistreating their citizens. All countries and, considering our traditional values and potential influence, especially the United States should follow a consistent policy of expressing views and shaping relations with foes and friends to support human rights, foster respect for the life, welfare, and safety from persecution of individuals, and foster individual rights and freedom.

When a government does mistreat its citizens we—individuals, human-rights groups, governments—must call the attention of perpetrators to basic rights and moral values and show that we consider their disregard to be of the greatest significance. We must do all that we can to make perpetrators aware of the costs of their atrocities to themselves, through diplomacy, boycotts, ostracism in the international community, and in other ways. We must make perpetrators aware that they won't escape punishment for their actions.

Through our positive acts, taking in refugees and reaching out to them, and through our attempts to inhibit human destructiveness, we can genuinely contribute to a "better world."

Notes on the Authors

LUCY NGUYEN-HONG-NHIEM was a teacher of French and a school administrator in Vietnam. She fled her native country and came to the United States in 1975. She received her M.A. and Ph.D. in Francophone literature from the University of Massachusetts at Amherst in 1982. She has since taught French at Smith, Mount Holyoke, and Amherst colleges, and is currently teaching Vietnamese literature at the University of Massachusetts at Amherst. She is author of "U.S.A.—Vietnam: Rencontres du 'Premier Type' (1819)" (*The Vietnam Forum,* Yale University, 1987), and "Introduction" and notes to *Blood Brothers,* a translation of *Freres de Sang* by Pham Van Ky (Yale University, Center for International and Area Studies, 1987). She works at the University of Massachusetts as an academic adviser to Asian and other bilingual minority students in the Bilingual Collegiate Program. She serves on the advisory boards of many voluntary agencies dealing with Southeast Asian refugees. She is the current vice-chair of the Governor's Advisory Council on Refugees and Immigrants.

JOEL MARTIN HALPERN has taught at the University of Massachusetts at Amherst since 1967 and was appointed professor in 1968. From 1956 to 1958 he was a provincial representative of the Community Development division of the American Aid Program in Laos, stationed in the royal capital of Luang Prabang (1957). Subsequently, he returned to Laos on research trips in 1959 and 1969. In the late 1960s he served as chair of the Mekong Committee of the Southeast Asia Development Advisory Group of the Asia Society in New York, which had as its aim the promotion of the United Nations Program for Mekong River Development. He has published monographs on Laotian political structure and on Lao society and economy (Yale University, Southeast Asian

Studies) as well as many articles. Most recently he has published a catalog of an exhibit of his photos on Laos and Lao-Americans with Sam Pettengill.

ERVIN STAUB is professor of psychology at the University of Massachusetts at Amherst. Since the 1960s, he has conducted research and published articles on the social, personality, and developmental origins and correlates of helping and altruism, and he has written a two-volume book on the subject. An additional, more recent focus of his work is on group violence. His forthcoming book (*The Roots of Evil: The Psychological and Cultural Origins of Genocide,* to be published early in 1989) explores the roots of war and torture and ways to reduce group violence.

DEIRDRE A. LING is vice chancellor for University Relations and Development at the University of Massachusetts at Amherst. She is an adjunct lecturer in the Women's Studies Department. Dr. Ling is an Asian American whose father immigrated to this country from China in 1929.

Student Contributors*

From Vietnam

Before DO MINH BANG's birth in Saigon in 1962, his parents had lived in their native North Vietnam, been evacuated to South Vietnam in 1954, and resettled in Phan Thiet, central Vietnam. Bang attended Catholic high school in Saigon and left his country, by boat, in 1980. His parents and three brothers remain there still. Bang stayed in an Indonesian refugee camp for six months and was then resettled in Nevada. In October 1980, he left Nevada for Boston, where he attended Brighton High School. He is now an electrical engineering major at the University of Massachusetts and will graduate in May 1989.

TA MINH TRI was born in Giadinh, South Vietnam, in June 1960 to a Chinese father and a Vietnamese mother, and he was educated in Vietnamese schools. In 1978, Tri and his three brothers left their homeland by boat and arrived at an Indonesian refugee camp. After eleven months in the camp, they resettled in Boston. Their parents remain in Vietnam. Tri majored in mechanical engineering at the University of Massachusetts and graduated in 1986. He works in Boston.

TRAN THI SANH was born in the coastal central Vietnamese town of Nha Trang in 1954. A teacher in her country, Sanh fled Vietnam by boat

*Student contributors are listed in the order of their appearance.

in 1980, leaving her mother and seven siblings behind. She was originally sent to a refugee camp in Kumato, in southern Japan, for nine months, after which time she was resettled in Haverhill, Massachusetts. She studied chemical engineering at the University of Massachusetts and received her degree in 1986. She presently works in Springfield, Massachusetts.

PHAN HUU THANH was born in the countryside of South Vietnam. His family moved to Saigon in 1962. Thanh left Vietnam in 1980; his family remains there. Thanh majored in electrical engineering at the University of Massachusetts and graduated in 1988.

NGUYEN HUNG ANH was born in Hue, the imperial capital of central Vietnam, in 1954. In 1979, Hung Anh left Hue by boat for the Philippines, where he stayed for fourteen months until he was resettled in Boston. Hung Anh attended the University of Massachusetts as an electrical engineering major and graduated in May 1986; he presently works at Atlas Engineering in Boston.

NGUYEN VAN NHAN, one of a family of eleven children, was born in Lang Co, a village of Hue, in 1964. Nhan left Vietnam by boat in 1980 and made his way to Hong Kong, where he stayed six months, and from there to Boston, Massachusetts. After a year of high school, Nhan attended the University of Massachusetts as a computer system engineering major and graduated in 1986. He now works in Boston.

HUYNH HUU HIEU was born in Vinh Binh, South Vietnam, in 1961; his family moved to Saigon in 1963. In 1979, Hieu left his country in a boat, stayed in a refugee camp in Malaysia where his father and brother joined him later. His mother and sister came to the United States in 1980, and the family resettled in Dorchester, Massachusetts. Hieu attended Brighton High School and then the University of Massachusetts as an electrical engineering student. Late in the summer of 1987, Hieu lost his parents, his sister, a cousin, and his fiancée in a tragedy that shocked the city of Boston. Hieu now owns a computer store in Boston.

LE TAN SI was born in Saigon in 1960. He left Vietnam by boat in 1979 and was resettled in Houston, Texas, in 1980. He later moved to Boston, where he attended Brighton High School. In 1982, he began his studies in math at the University of Massachusetts. He has graduated and works in Boston.

DANG HONG LOAN was born in Saigon in 1961. Her father was an army officer. Loan attended a Catholic high school in Giadinh (a neighboring town to Saigon). She left Vietnam with her grandmother and her aunt's family in 1975. They were resettled in Houston, Texas. Her mother and two young brothers had left earlier and are now in the Philippines. Her father remained in Vietnam. Loan came to the University of Massachusetts in 1980 and graduated in 1985 with an electrical engineering degree. Loan and her husband are now working in Dallas, Texas.

LAM PHU was born to Chinese parents in Banmethuot, in the highlands of central Vietnam, in 1962. The tenth of eleven children, Phu and his siblings attended Chinese and Vietnamese schools. Phu's father died in 1977; two years later, Phu and two brothers left Vietnam and, after spending a year in an Indonesian refugee camp, resettled in Boston. Four years later, their mother was reunited with them in the United States under the provisions of the Orderly Departure Program. Phu is now a senior at the University of Massachusetts, majoring in engineering.

NGUYEN HUU CHUNG was born in Saigon in 1965 to North Vietnamese parents. His family's journey to the United States was done piecemeal: his father and a brother came in 1975, followed by Chung, a sister, and another brother in 1980. In 1982, two more sisters joined them. Finally, in 1986, the entire family was reunited when Chung's mother and two remaining brothers were able to come to the United States under the Orderly Departure Program. They now live in Ludlow, Massachusetts. Chung is a graduate of the University of Massachusetts, and has a degree in electrical engineering.

From Cambodia

PHYRUN KHATH was born in Takeo on August 3, 1967, and he lived in Phnom Penh with his uncle's family. When they were evacuated from the city to the countryside in 1975, Phyrun became separated from his brother and from his uncle's family. He arrived in Thailand in 1979 and stayed in a refugee camp where he was sponsored by a Cambodian family that brought him with them to Indonesia and then to the United States. They were originally resettled in Williamsburg, Massachusetts, and later moved to Northampton, where Phyrun attended high school. Phyrun began his studies at the University of Massachusetts in September 1987.

ROEUN CHEA was born in Takeo, in rural Cambodia, in 1968. As a young boy, he did not attend school. In 1975, he was put in a children's labor camp, where he stayed until 1979. He walked from the camp to Battambang, and then on to Thailand; the trip took him two months. He stayed in the Khao I Dang refugee camp for three years, until he was sponsored by the

Unaccompanied Minors Program of Lutheran Services in Amherst. He now lives with an American foster family. He is a sophomore at the University of Massachusetts at Amherst.

BORETH SUN was born in Battambang in April 1965, one of seven children of a businessman and housewife. In 1975, the family was forced to leave Battambang by order of the Khmer Rouge; Boreth was taken from his family and placed in a children's labor camp. After three years in the camp, he fled to the jungle with two of his sisters. He later escaped to Thailand and lived in a refugee camp for four years. In 1983, sponsored by the Unaccompanied Minors Program of Lutheran Services, he came to live with a foster family in Amherst. Boreth now attends the University of Massachusetts as a fourth-year human services major.

CHANTHOUK ROS was born in Battambang in 1967. Along with her parents and five siblings, she walked to Thailand. Two of her sisters were left behind. Her family stayed in Khao I Dang for three years and was resettled in Boston in 1983. Chanthouk attended South Boston and Brighton high schools before she came to the University of Massachusetts in September 1987.

HONG TAING was born in Phnom Penh in 1967, to a Chinese father and Cambodian mother. His parents owned a business in that city before they were forced to move to the countryside by the Khmer Rouge. In 1979 the whole family walked to Thailand but was pushed back to Cambodia. Hong tried to leave again, and he made it to Khao I Dang where he stayed for fifteen months. His family remained in Cambodia. Hong came to the United States in 1983 under the sponsorship of a Virginia Baptist church. He moved to Northampton, Massachusetts in 1984 to join his relatives. He attended Northampton High School and is currently a second-year student at the University of Massachusetts.

MARK GRAY, the author of the essay on Vannorath Sarin's life, met Vannorath in an anthropology class at the University of Massachusetts. Mark graduated from the University of Massachusetts in 1986 with a degree in political science; he then studied Chinese and taught English in Taipei, Taiwan. Mark is now in Bangkok, Thailand, where he is learning Thai and earning a master's degree in political science. He is a native of Massachusetts, born on March 4, 1963.

SRENG KOUCH was born to Chinese parents in Kompongcham on August 25, 1967. He came to the United States in 1980 with his parents and six siblings; his family now lives in Lynn, where, as they had in Cambodia, they own a small business. Sreng is a senior at the University of Massachusetts, studying computer and information science.

HORNG KOUCH was born in Kompongcham, Cambodia, in 1969. She did not attend school in her homeland. She and her family walked four days and three nights to get to a refugee camp in Thailand. After eight months in Khao I Dang, she and her family were resettled in Lynn, Massachusetts. She is now a University of Massachusetts sophomore.

VIBORA LIM was born in Phnom Penh on May 2, 1966. His mother had been born in Cambodia to Chinese parents; his father, a Cambodian, was at that time a commander in the army. In 1975, Vibora, his parents, and his brother and sister drove to Thailand; there they lived in a refugee camp for two months. They were relocated to Los Angeles, and, in 1976, moved to Boston. Vibora is in his fourth year at the University of Massachusetts, studying management.

MAX HARTSHORNE, who contributed the essay on the experiences of Chard Huon, was born in Brooklyn, New York, in 1958. Max has worked extensively in the field of journalism, as both author and editor. Fascinated by the histories of so many young Cambodian refugees, Max chose to investigate more thoroughly the life of Chard Huon. He attended the University of Massachusetts from 1984 to 1986, majoring in English.

From Laos

NILANDONE PATHAMMAVONG was born in Vientiane, Laos, on July 8, 1964. In 1979 she and her family left their home for a Thai refugee camp. Two years later, they resettled in Manchester, Connecticut, where they lived for three years before moving to Springfield, Massachusetts. Nilandone graduated from the University of Massachusetts in 1988 with an industrial engineering degree.

CHANTHAVA CHANTAVONG was born in Savannakhet, Laos, on September 6, 1965. She and her parents, two brothers, and sister came to the United States in 1979, resettling initially in Maryland and then moving to Greenfield, Massachusetts, two years later. Chanthava is a fourth-year bilingual and elementary multicultural education major at the University of Massachusetts at Amherst.

CHANTHA SOUVANNA was born in Vientiane on December 23, 1964; his father was a military man and his mother, a weaver. In March 1979,

Chantha swam across the Mekong River and arrived in Thailand, where he stayed in a refugee camp for a year. His mother, brother, and sister were later able to join him in the camp. The family came to the United States in December 1980 and were resettled in Weston, Massachusetts. Chantha attended Weston High School and the University of Massachusetts. He works in Needham, Massachusetts.

LAMTHIANE INTHIRATH was born in Savannakhet on August 10, 1964, to a Thai father and Lao mother. Lamthiane left Laos in 1975; with her parents and four siblings, she walked along and then crossed the Mekong River into Thailand. Her family lived there for four years, until they were resettled in Leominster, Massachusetts. Lamthiane attended the University of Massachusetts as a zoology major. She is married, has a child, and is working in a dairy lab in Springfield, Massachusetts.